101
best campsites
for nature lovers

2015

alan
rogers

Compiled by: Alan Rogers Travel Ltd

Designed by: Vine Design Ltd

© Alan Rogers Travel Ltd 2014

Published by: Alan Rogers Travel Ltd,
Spelmonden Old Oast, Goudhurst, Kent TN17 1HE
Tel: 01580 214000 www.alanrogers.com

British Library Cataloguing-in-Publication Data:
A catalogue record for this book is
available from the British Library.

ISBN 978-1-909057-58-6

Printed in Great Britain by
Stephens & George Print Group

While every effort is taken to ensure the accuracy of the information
given in this book, no liability can be accepted by the authors or
publishers for any loss, damage or injury caused by errors in, or
omissions from, the information given.

Contents

Welcome to the Alan Rogers
'101' guides

The Alan Rogers guides have been helping campers and caravanners make informed decisions about their holiday destinations since 1968. Today, whether online or in print, Alan Rogers still provides an independent, impartial view, with detailed reports, on each campsite.

With so much unfiltered, unqualified information freely available, the Alan Rogers perspective is invaluable to make sure you make the right choice for your holiday.

What is the '101' series?

At Alan Rogers, we know that readers have many and diverse interests, hobbies and particular requirements. And we know that our guides, featuring a total of some 3,000 campsites, can provide a bewildering choice from which it can be difficult to produce a shortlist of possible holiday destinations.

The Alan Rogers 101 guides are devised as a means of presenting a realistic, digestible number of great campsites, featured because of their suitability to a given theme.

This book remains first and foremost an authoritative guide to excellent campsites with an emphasis on natural surroundings and where you'll be close to nature.

101 Best campsites
for nature

More than any other form of holiday, camping is closely linked with nature. Whether you trace the links back to primitive forms of camping, such as the Native Indians or even the Scout movement, all require an understanding of our natural surroundings and a dependence on it.

Today, for most people, the main appeal of a camping holiday is that link with nature – however it may manifest itself.

We may dream wistfully of childhood tents in the garden, waking up to the dawn chorus after a night of toasted marshmallows and fireside stories. We may dream of life in the wigwams of the North American prairies, at one with nature. We may dream of taking the caravan deep into some picture postcard location, or unpacking the surfboard on some wild, unspoilt beach.

Wherever we look for nature, and whatever we want from that quest, camping 'amidst nature' invariably brings a unique sense of wellbeing and a taste of a simpler life.

This guide highlights 101 campsites which all, in differing ways, offer a taste of nature. Whether nestling in wild dunes by the sea or surrounded by alpine meadows, you'll find a campsite which will provide you with a taste of the natural world.

Alan Rogers – in search
of 'the best'

Alan Rogers himself started off with the very specific aim of providing people with the necessary information to allow them to make an informed decision about their holiday destination. Today we still do that with a range of guides that now covers Europe's best campsites in 27 countries. We work with campsites all day, every day. We visit campsites for inspection purposes (or even just for pleasure!). We know campsites 'inside out'.

We know which campsites would suit active families; which are great for get-away-from-it-all couples; we know which campsites are planning super new pool complexes; which campsites offer a fantastic menu in their on-site restaurant; which campsites allow you to launch a small boat from their slipway; which campsites have a decent playing area for kicking a ball around; which campsites have flat, grassy pitches and which have solid hard standings.

All Alan Rogers guides (and our website) are respected for their independent, impartial and honest assessment. The reviews are prose-based, without overuse of indecipherable icons and symbols. Our simple aim is to help guide you to a campsite that best matches your requirements – often quite difficult in today's age of information overload.

What is
the best?

The criteria we use when inspecting and selecting sites are numerous, but the most important by far is the question of good quality. People want different things from their choice of campsite, so campsite 'styles' vary dramatically: from small peaceful campsites in the heart of the countryside, to 'all singing, all dancing' sites in popular seaside resorts.

The size of the site, whether it's part of a chain or privately owned, makes no difference in terms of it being required to meet our exacting standards in respect of its quality and it being 'fit for purpose'. In other words, irrespective of the size of the site, or the number of facilities it offers, we consider and evaluate the welcome, the pitches, the sanitary facilities, the cleanliness, the general maintenance and even the location.

Expert
opinions

We rely on our dedicated team of Site Assessors, all of whom are experienced campers, caravanners or motorcaravanners, to visit and recommend campsites. Each year they travel around Europe inspecting new campsites for Alan Rogers and re-inspecting the existing ones.

When planning
your holiday...

A holiday should always be a relaxing affair, and a campsite-based holiday particularly so. Our aim is for you to find the ideal campsite for your holiday, one that suits your requirements. All Alan Rogers guides provide a wealth of information, including some details supplied by campsite owners themselves, and the following points may help ensure that you plan a successful holiday.

Find out more

An Alan Rogers reference number (eg FR12345) is given for each campsite and can be useful for finding more information and pictures online at www.alanrogers.com. Simply enter this number in the 'Campsite Search' field on the Home page.

Campsite descriptions

We aim to convey an idea of its general appearance, 'feel' and features, with details of pitch numbers, electricity, hardstandings etc.

Facilities

We list specific information on the site's facilities and amenities and, where available, the dates when these facilities are open (if not for the whole season). Much of this information is as supplied to us and may be subject to change. Should any particular activity or aspect of the campsite be important to you, it is always worth discussing with the campsite before you travel.

Swimming pools

Opening dates, any charges and levels of supervision are provided where we have been notified. In some countries (notably France) there is a regulation whereby Bermuda-style shorts may not be worn in swimming pools (for health and hygiene reasons). It is worth ensuring that you do take 'proper' swimming trunks with you.

Charges

Those given are the latest provided to us, usually 2014 prices, and should be viewed as a guide only.

Toilet blocks

Unless we comment otherwise, toilet blocks will be equipped with a reasonable number of British style WCs, washbasins and hot showers in cubicles. We also assume that there will be an identified chemical toilet disposal point, and that the campsite will provide water and waste water drainage points and bin areas. If not the case, we comment. We do mention certain features that some readers find important: washbasins in cubicles, facilities for babies, facilities for those with disabilities and motorcaravan service points.

Reservations

Necessary for high season (roughly mid July to mid August) in popular holiday areas (i.e. beach resorts). You can reserve many sites via our own Alan Rogers Travel Service or through other tour operators. Remember, many sites are closed all winter and you may struggle to get an answer.

Telephone numbers

All numbers assume that you are phoning from within the country in question. From the UK or Ireland, dial 00, then the country's prefix (e.g. France is 33), then the campsite number given, but dropping the first '0'.

Opening dates

Dates given are those provided to us and can alter before the start of the season. If you intend to visit shortly after a published opening date, or shortly before the closing date, it is wise to check that it will actually be open at the time required. Similarly some sites operate a restricted service during the low season, only opening some of their facilities (e.g. swimming pools) during the main season; where we know about this, and have the relevant dates, we indicate it – again if you are at all doubtful it is wise to check.

Accommodation

Over recent years, more and more campsites have added high quality mobile homes, chalets, lodges, gîtes and more. Where applicable we indicate what is available and you'll find details online.

Special Offers

Some campsites have taken the opportunity to highlight a special offer. This is arranged by them and for clarification please contact the campsite direct.

What
is nature...?

Nature means different things to different people. When camping (in any of its forms) it might mean a stunning, unspoilt setting; it might mean an absence of unnecessary facilities and a campsite stripped of technology. Others might prefer to drink in the exhilarating views, savour new experiences and still be able to check emails!

How
do you camp?

With over 30,000 campsites in Europe, there are campsites in all kinds of natural environments. (Not to mention some – not featured in this guide – which have nothing natural about them at all).

Woodland camping

Camping among trees, or in clearings, always brings a very special atmosphere. The broadleaf forests of England conjure sentiments somewhere between Robin Hood and Squirrel Nutkin. The scented pine forests of Aquitaine have a definite 'Frenchness' about them, while the Bavarian forests evoke all kinds of Hansel and Gretel memories. When camping under a tree canopy you'll feel up close and personal with nature.

Coastal camping

The salty, fresh air of the seaside and drifting dunes or muddy estuaries always convey a natural, cleansing purity. Campsites might be right on the beach or set inland slightly but there are always plenty of educational activities for children.

Waterside camping

Campsites adjacent to rivers and lakes have their own natural charm. Shady banks, shallow margins, tumbling rapids all create a unique environment for rare wildlife and a fascinating playground for adults and children alike.

Mountain camping

Of course you don't have to be on some icy windswept peak in order to experience the glorious vistas, the clear air, the stillness and singular flora and fauna that come with camping at height. From England's craggy Peak District, to the Pyrenees, via the Alps to Scandinavian peaks and Italian Dolomites and beyond....

Rural camping

Those campsites based on a farm or amidst an agricultural landscape appeal to those who enjoy the feeling of space and freedom to roam that comes from big skies, rolling countryside and distant horizons.

Officially,
natural

The now well understood problem of recognising areas of outstanding natural beauty and interest, encouraging visitors to visit them, and then managing the impact caused by large numbers of visitors is largely managed by Europe's National Parks. Well over 350 of them in fact and between them featuring a huge range of landscapes, from alpine to forest, from lakeland to grassland, from steppe to tidal basin.

The Europarc Federation brings together Europe's protected areas, unifying national parks, regional parks, nature parks and eco reserves in nearly 40 countries. The PAN Parks organisation represents some of the most important wilderness areas, developing sustainable tourism while protecting fragile regions.

The National Parks of Europe
– an overview

- The Netherlands' 20 national parks include Hooge Veluwe Natural Park, the largest, whose forests, shifting sand dunes and heather-clad moors protect roe deer, boar and numerous species of birds.

- Ireland's six national parks, include Killarney National Park, in County Kerry, famed for its lake-studded mountains, and Connemara National Park with its lunar landscape of peat bogs.

- The UK's 15 national parks range from the wilds of Exmoor to the 16 lakes of the Lake District. Wales' Brecon Beacons, Pembrokeshire Coast and Snowdonia are truly dramatic, as are Scotland's parks of the Cairngorms and Loch Lomond.

- Germany's 14 national parks vary from the high mountains of Berchtesgaden to the beech forests of Eifel.

- Austria's seven national parks cover 900 square miles of alpine massifs, forests and steppes.

- France's seven national parks are all uniquely dramatic landscapes, including world-class sites in the Alps, Cévennes and the Pyrenees.

- Hungary's ten parks include the famous Balaton High Country National Park.

- Sweden has 29 parks, all with huge mountains rising from glacial lakes, rivers and marshes and vast beech forests.

- Norway's 25 parks include lofty peaks, glaciers, evergreen forests and lakes.

- Spain's 13 parks, such as Picos de Europa and Ordesa in the Pyrenees, are a last refuge for endangered species.

- Portugal has 13 parks, including the home of the Iberian wolf and the royal eagle.

- Italy's 23 parks range from the mountainous Val d'Aoste, the Italian Alps and Pollino National Park, home to wolves and 40 metre tall pines, to Abruzzo with its endangered bears, chamois and wolves. Vesuvius National Park needs little introduction.

Activities
in nature

Being 'out there', immersed in nature, provides scope for all kinds of activities. It may take a while to shed the day-to-day habits and routines of daily life but an impromptu kite flying session, or an exploratory ramble along an enticing path can soon get you in the swing.

Two legs good,
two wheels good

Walking and hiking are ever popular activities, being environmentally friendly and convenient. Cycle hire is often available and many campsites endeavour to make the most of their surroundings with marked trails. Indeed some of France's famous long distance paths (grandes randonnées) pass beside or even through some French campsites.

Children
and nature

Children and nature go, well, hand in hand. Most youngsters are intrigued by bugs and mini beasts and something vaguely educational is also great fun and simple entertainment. Guessing the Petals, is always a winner: excellent for quiet concentration and awareness of nature, the aim is simply to guess the number of petals on a selection of flowers.

With nature trails, birdlife, butterflies, squirrels, equestrian trails, perhaps rockpools, there's always something to engage, fascinate and teach. And of course, doing nothing has its own rewards too: when with young children try and do the unusual: take a short stroll, stop and stand for five minutes, listening and watching. You'll be amazed at what you observe together.

A natural
approach

A number of campsite chains or marketing groups deliberately set out their stall to attract nature-lovers. Whereas some campsites have embraced the latest developments in infrastructure, groups like Sites et Paysages and Flower Camping have eschewed massive aqua parks in favour of enhancing their environmental and natural settings. Huttopia, working with the French Forestry Commission, offers a progressive style of camping which is actually 'retro' in its principles: think environmental commitment, small uncommercialised campsites with large 120 sq.m. pitches and a relaxed feel. The Camping and Caravanning Club, with their Forest Holidays, offer woodland holidays with real eco-ethics. And some like Kawan Villages have integrated 'nature' activities into their on-site programmes, and worked hard on developing walking and cycling routes.

Enjoy...!

Whether you're an 'old hand' or are contemplating your first trip, a regular reader of our Guides or a new 'convert', we wish you well in your travels and hope we have been able to help in some way. We are, of course, also out and about ourselves, visiting sites, talking to owners and readers, and generally checking on standards and new developments. We hope to bump into you!

Wishing you thoroughly enjoyable camping and caravanning in 2015 – favoured by good weather of course!

The Alan Rogers Team

A natural
balance

For many ecologically minded campsites 'low impact' is a mantra. The environmental schemes like Bellamy and Clef Verte are just part of the bigger picture: the cycle of the seasons, the inter-reliance between plant and insect, predator and prey, crops and birdlife, fruit and wildlife, forest canopy and the eco-system of the woodland floor below. All this is important in maintaining natural balance and a thriving habitat. And campsites, being a vital link in a local community, form part of an unbroken chain too. Well managed campsites will value this, hence their emphasis on slow food, reduced food miles, locally produced artisan goods and the like.

Ferienparadies Natterer See

Natterer See 1, A-6161 Natters (Tirol)
t: 051 254 6732   e: info@natterersee.com
alanrogers.com/AU0060   www.natterersee.com

Accommodation: ☑ Pitch   ○ Mobile home/chalet   ○ Hotel/B&B   ☑ Apartment

In a quiet location arranged around two lakes and set amidst beautiful alpine scenery, this site founded in 1930 is renowned as one of Austria's top sites. Over the last few years many improvements have been carried out and pride of place goes to the innovative, award-winning, multifunctional building at the entrance to the site. This contains all of the sanitary facilities expected of a top site, including a special section for children, private bathrooms to rent and also a dog bath. The reception, shop, café/bar/bistro and cinema are on the ground floor, and on the upper floor is a panoramic lounge. Almost all of the 235 pitches are for tourers. They are terraced, set on gravel/grass, all have electricity and most offer a splendid view of the mountains. The site's lakeside restaurant with bar and large terrace has a good menu and is the ideal place to spend the evening. With a bus every hour and the city centre only 19 minutes away this is also a good site from which to visit Innsbruck.

You might like to know

This is a great base for a hiking holiday with many accompanied walks available. These include a free shuttle, free hiking boot and day pack rental and the service of an accredited guide.

☑ Environmental accreditation
☑ Reduced energy/water consumption policy
☑ Recycling and reusing policy
☑ Information about walking and cycling
☑ Footpaths within 500 m. of the site
☑ Fishing within 1 km.
○ Riding or pony trekking within 1 km.
☑ Direct river or lake access
☑ Area of outstanding natural beauty or National Park within 10 km.
○ Wildlife haven (on site or within 1 km)
○ Public transport
○ Dogs welcome

Facilities: The large sanitary block has underfloor heating, some private cabins, plus excellent facilities for babies, children and disabled visitors. Laundry facilities. Motorcaravan services. Fridge box hire. Bar. Restaurant and takeaway with at least one open all year. Pizzeria. Good shop. Playgrounds. Children's activity programme. Child minding (day nursery) in high season. Sports field. Archery. Youth room with games, pool and billiards. TV room with Sky. Open-air cinema. Mountain bike hire. Aquapark (1/5-30/9). Surf bikes and pedaloes. Canoes and mini sailboats for rent. Fishing. Extensive daily entertainment programme (mid May-mid Oct). Dogs are not accepted in high season (July/Aug). WiFi (charged). Off site: Tennis and minigolf nearby. Riding 6 km. Golf 12 km.

Open: All year.

Directions: From Inntal autobahn (A12) take Brenner autobahn (A13) as far as Innsbruck-sud/Natters exit (no. 3). Turn left by Shell petrol station onto B182 to Natters. At roundabout take first exit and immediately right again and follow signs to site 4 km. Do not use sat nav for final approach to site, follow camping signs.
GPS: 47.23755, 11.34201

Charges guide

Per unit incl. 2 persons and electricity	€ 24,45 - € 33,25
extra person	€ 6,10 - € 9,00
child (under 13 yrs)	€ 4,80 - € 6,50
dog (excl. July/Aug)	€ 4,50 - € 5,00

Special weekly, winter, summer or Christmas packages.

Facilities: The sanitary facilities are first class and include ten bathrooms to rent for private use. Baby room. Facilities for disabled visitors. Dog shower. Washing machine and dryer. Ski room. Motorcaravan service point. Small shop. Good value restaurant. Playground. Bicycle hire. Fishing. WiFi over site (charged). Apartments to rent. Renovated fitness and play rooms. Off site: Riding 200 m. Tiroler farmhouse museum 1 km. Kramsach 3 km. Rattenberg 4 km. Swarovski Kristallwelten. Zillertal. Innsbruck. Kufstein.

Open: All year.

Directions: From A12 take Kramsach exit and follow signs for Zu den Seen past Camping Krummsee and Stadlerhof along northern shore of lake, then right at crossroads. All clearly signed. Camping Seehof (300 m) is the first campsite you reach. New driveway and reception on the left.

GPS: 47.46196, 11.90713

Charges guide

Per unit incl. 2 persons and electricity	€ 17,30 - € 26,30
extra person	€ 4,60 - € 6,90
child (2-14 yrs)	€ 3,20 - € 4,70
dog	€ 3,00 - € 3,50

Camping & Appartements Seehof

Reintalersee, Moosen 42, A-6233 Kramsach (Tirol)
t: 053 376 3541 e: info@camping-seehof.com
alanrogers.com/AU0065 www.camping-seehof.com

Accommodation: ☑ Pitch ○ Mobile home/chalet ○ Hotel/B&B ☑ Apartment

Camping Seehof is a family run site and excellent in every respect. It is situated in a marvellous sunny and peaceful location on the eastern shores of the Reintalersee. The site's comfortable restaurant has a terrace with lake and mountain views and serves local dishes as well as homemade cakes and ice cream. The site is in two areas: a small one next to the lake is ideal for sunbathing, the other larger one adjoins the excellent sanitary block. There are 170 pitches, 140 of which are for touring (20 tent pitches), served by good access roads and with 16A electricity (Europlug) and TV points; 100 pitches are fully serviced, with more being upgraded every year. Seehof provides an ideal starting point for walking, cycling and riding (with a riding stable nearby) and skiing in winter. The Alpbachtal Seenland card is available without cost at reception and allows free bus transport and free daily entry to many worthwhile attractions in the region.

You might like to know

The Alpbachtal Seenland card enables campsite guests to take advantage of a wide variety of activities in the area, either at a discounted rate or free of charge.

- ☑ Environmental accreditation
- ☑ Reduced energy/water consumption policy
- ☑ Recycling and reusing policy
- ☑ Information about walking and cycling
- ☑ Footpaths within 500 m. of the site
- ☑ Fishing within 1 km.
- ☑ Riding or pony trekking within 1 km.
- ☑ Direct river or lake access
- ☑ Area of outstanding natural beauty or National Park within 10 km.
- ○ Wildlife haven (on site or within 1 km)
- ☑ Public transport
- ☑ Dogs welcome

Facilities: One new, centrally located toilet block (heated) with toilets, washbasins (open style and in cabins) and free, controllable hot showers. Bathroom. Washing machine. Dryer. Bar/restaurant with takeaway and covered terrace (closed May and Nov). Fishing. Skate ramp. Swimming pond with small beach. Full activity programme for all in high season. WiFi over site (charged). Off site: Riding 2 km. Golf 25 km.

Open: All year.

Directions: From the A12, take exit 132 at Imst and continue south to Arzl and Wenns; continue toward St. Leonhard. Site is signed to the right 4 km. south of Wenns. (Important: set sat nav to Wenns not Jerzens).

GPS: 47.14253, 10.746483

Charges guide

Per unit incl. 2 persons and electricity	€ 19,00 - € 27,00
extra person	€ 6,50 - € 7,50
child (4-16 yrs)	€ 4,00 - € 5,00
dog	€ 2,00

Austria – Jerzens

Mountain Camp Pitztal

Niederhof 206, A-6474 Jerzens (Tirol)
t: 054 148 7571   e: info@mountain-camp.at
alanrogers.com/AU0085   www.mountain-camp.at

Accommodation: ☑ Pitch   ○ Mobile home/chalet   ○ Hotel/B&B   ☑ Apartment

This is a small, unspoiled family run site set among the mountains in the Pitztal. It is an ideal base for walks in the Tirolean mountains and for mountain bike tours on the numerous paths through the woods and on the Schotterpiste and Wildspitze, the highest mountain in the Tirol. Each of the 38 open plan pitches has 13A electricity, water, waste water and gas points. The pitches are laid out on level, rectangular fields on a grass and gravel base, with gravel access roads. There are beautiful views of the mountains on all sides and an Alpine stream feeds the lake and fish ponds. To one end of the site is a welcoming restaurant with covered terrace for meals and drinks with views of the swimming and fishing ponds. To the front of the site is an area for beach volleyball with opportunities for basketball and a skate ramp as well. The restaurant serves fresh fish daily and walking and cycling tours are organised. A free shuttle bus runs from the site gate to the ski slopes.

You might like to know

This site is an ideal starting point for hiking in the Tyrolean mountains, and the closest mountain (Hochzeiger) can be accessed by cable car.

- ☑ Environmental accreditation
- ☑ Reduced energy/water consumption policy
- ☑ Recycling and reusing policy
- ☑ Information about walking and cycling
- ☑ Footpaths within 500 m. of the site
- ☑ Fishing within 1 km.
- ○ Riding or pony trekking within 1 km.
- ○ Direct river or lake access
- ☑ Area of outstanding natural beauty or National Park within 10 km.
- ○ Wildlife haven (on site or within 1 km)
- ○ Public transport
- ☑ Dogs welcome

Facilities: Toilet facilities are clean, heated and modern with free showers. No facilities for disabled visitors. Washing machines and dryers. Motorcaravan service point. Shop (July/Aug). Excellent restaurant/bar (1/6-1/9). Small play area. WiFi (charged). Swimming in adjoining lake. Lakeside games field. Off site: The historic town of Lienz 5 km. Plenty of things to do in the area (information found in a copy of the Osttirol brochure supplied to all campsite visitors).

Open: 20 May - 14 September.

Directions: Site is 5 km. east of Lienz. Take the B100 and the B318. 1.5 km. past Tristach, turn right (signed) and climb the steep (1:10) hill for 1 km. to the site.

GPS: 46.80601, 12.80307

Charges guide

Per unit incl. 2 persons and electricity € 30,00 - € 34,50	
extra person € 8,00	
child (4-15 yrs) € 4,50	
dog € 3,00	

No credit cards.

Campingplatz Seewiese

Tristachersee 2, A-9900 Lienz-Tristach (Tirol)
t: 048 526 9767 e: seewiese@hotmail.com
alanrogers.com/AU0185 www.campingtirol.com

Accommodation: ☑ Pitch ○ Mobile home/chalet ○ Hotel/B&B ○ Apartment

High above the village of Tristach and 5 km. from Lienz, this is a perfect location for a peaceful and relaxing holiday or as a base for exploring the Dolomite region. Situated amongst giant conifers and surrounded by snow-capped mountains, the site offers everyone a view of the volcanic Lake Tristachsee. The 110 pitches all have 6A electricity (long leads necessary for some) and the 14 pitches for motorcaravans near reception each have electricity, water and drainage. Caravans are sited on a gently sloping field which has level areas although pitches are unmarked and unnumbered. At the bottom of this field is the lake which is used for swimming. There are many opportunities for sporting activities including kayaking, rafting, mountain biking, climbing and paragliding. The more sedate may be happy with walking or golf, both of which can also be found nearby. Younger guests will have great fun exploring in the woods.

You might like to know

There is a free, daily shuttle bus to Linz, the regional capital.

- ☑ Environmental accreditation
- ☑ Reduced energy/water consumption policy
- ☑ Recycling and reusing policy
- ☑ Information about walking and cycling
- ☑ Footpaths within 500 m. of the site
- ☑ Fishing within 1 km.
- ○ Riding or pony trekking within 1 km.
- ☑ Direct river or lake access
- ☑ Area of outstanding natural beauty or National Park within 10 km.
- ○ Wildlife haven (on site or within 1 km)
- ☑ Public transport
- ☑ Dogs welcome

Facilities: Sanitary building. Laundry facilities and drying room. Solarium. Swimming pool. Internet. WiFi throughout (free). Charcoal barbecues not permitted. Off site: Abtenau 2.5 km. (about 25 minutes walk). Skiing 2.5 km. Riding 8 km. Hallstättersee and salt mines 30 km. The Panorama Strasse.

Open: All year.

Directions: Abtenau is 34 km. southeast of Salzburg. From A10 exit 28 (Golling), take B162 east for 14 km. and site is signed to the left 2.5 km. before Abtenau (sat nav is unreliable).

GPS: 47.585704, 13.324635

Charges guide

Per unit incl. 2 persons
(electricity on meter) € 21,20 - € 28,00

extra person € 6,00 - € 7,50

child (3-15 yrs) € 3,50 - € 4,00

dog € 2,50

No credit cards.

Austria – Abtenau

Oberwötzlhof Camp

Erlfeld 37, A-5441 Abtenau (Salzburg)
t: 062 432 698 e: oberwoetzlhof@sbg.at
alanrogers.com/AU0262 www.oberwoetzlhof-camp.at

Accommodation: ⦿ Pitch ◯ Mobile home/chalet ◯ Hotel/B&B ◯ Apartment

High up in the Lammertal Valley is this small, hilltop farm site with attractive views of the surrounding mountains. Part of a working farm, it has a total of 70 pitches, of which 40 are for touring units. All are serviced with 10A electricity, water and drainage. The site is quiet at night, and dark, so a torch would be useful. The small, fenced swimming pool (10x5 m) is unheated, and has paved surrounds. The site has attractive sanitary facilities, completed in 2010, and together with its rural location and a friendly atmosphere is a good site for those seeking some peace and quiet. Drinks and ices are available during the summer season. Places to visit should include Postalm, real alpine meadow country with some excellent walking (brochure from reception). There are many opportunities for rafting, hydrospeeding, canyoning, paragliding and mountain biking in the area. No English is spoken.

You might like to know

There are 300 km. of signposted and well kept walking, hiking and mountain trails in and around Abtenau, of which 200 km. are described as 'easy'.

- ☑ Environmental accreditation
- ☑ Reduced energy/water consumption policy
- ☑ Recycling and reusing policy
- ☑ Information about walking and cycling
- ☑ Footpaths within 500 m. of the site
- ◯ Fishing within 1 km.
- ◯ Riding or pony trekking within 1 km.
- ◯ Direct river or lake access
- ☑ Area of outstanding natural beauty or National Park within 10 km.
- ◯ Wildlife haven (on site or within 1 km)
- ◯ Public transport
- ☑ Dogs welcome

Naturpark Schluga Seecamping

A-9620 Hermagor (Carinthia)
t: 042 822 051 e: camping@schluga.com
alanrogers.com/AU0450 www.schluga.com

Accommodation: ⦿ Pitch ⦿ Mobile home/chalet ○ Hotel/B&B ⦿ Apartment

This site is pleasantly situated on natural wooded hillside. It is about 300 m. from a small lake with clean water, where the site has a beach of coarse sand and a large grassy meadow where inflatable boats can be kept. There is also a small bar and a sunbathing area for naturists, although this is not a naturist site. The 250 pitches for touring units are on individual, level terraces, many with light shade and all with electricity (8-16A). One hundred and fifty-four pitches also have water, drainage and satellite TV and a further 47 pitches are occupied by a tour operator. English is spoken. This part of Carinthia is a little off the beaten track but the site still becomes full in season. Close by is Schluga Camping, under the same ownership, which is open all year. From both sites, there are views of the mountains, snowcapped in early summer. Many walks and attractive car drives are available in the area.

Facilities: Four heated modern toilet blocks are well constructed, with some washbasins in cabins and family washrooms for rent. Facilities for disabled campers. Washing machines and dryer. Motorcaravan services. Shop (20/5-10/9). Restaurant/bar by entrance and takeaway (all 20/5-10/9). Playground. Room for young people and children. Films. Kiosk and bar with terrace at beach. Surf school. Pedalo and canoe hire. Aqua jump and Iceberg. Pony rides. Bicycle hire. Weekly activity programme with mountain walks and climbs. Internet point. WiFi over site (charged). Off site: Fishing and sailing 200 m. Riding 12 km. Golf 16 km. Tennis (indoor and outdoor).

Open: 10 May - 20 September.

Directions: Site is on the B111 road (Villach-Hermagor) 6 km. east of Hermagor town.

GPS: 46.63184, 13.44654

Charges guide

Per unit incl. 2 persons and electricity	€ 18,10 - € 33,75
extra person	€ 5,60 - € 8,85
child (5-14 yrs)	€ 4,00 - € 6,00
dog	€ 3,00 - € 3,90

You might like to know

Every Tuesday, the site organises mountain rambles for beginners. These excursions include trips to the mountains in the Gail Valley and the Carnic ranges.

- ⦿ Environmental accreditation
- ⦿ Reduced energy/water consumption policy
- ⦿ Recycling and reusing policy
- ⦿ Information about walking and cycling
- ⦿ Footpaths within 500 m. of the site
- ⦿ Fishing within 1 km.
- ○ Riding or pony trekking within 1 km.
- ⦿ Direct river or lake access
- ⦿ Area of outstanding natural beauty or National Park within 10 km.
- ○ Wildlife haven (on site or within 1 km)
- ⦿ Public transport
- ⦿ Dogs welcome

Camping Baalse Hei

Roodhuisstraat 10, B-2300 Turnhout (Antwerp)
t: 014 448 470 e: info@baalsehei.be
alanrogers.com/BE0660 www.baalsehei.be

Accommodation: ✔ Pitch ✔ Mobile home/chalet ○ Hotel/B&B ○ Apartment

The Campine is an area covering three quarters of the Province of Antwerp, noted for its nature reserves, pine forests, meadows and streams and is ideal for walking and cycling, while Turnhout itself is an interesting old town. Baalse Hei, a long established, friendly site, has 469 pitches including a separate touring area of 71 large grass pitches (all with 16A electricity, TV connections and shared water point), thoughtfully developed with trees and bushes. Cars are parked away from, but near the pitches. Large motorcaravans can be accommodated (phone first to check availability). There is also accommodation to rent. It is 100 m. from the edge of the field to the modern, heated, sanitary building. There is a small lake for swimming with a beach, a boating lake and a large fishing lake (on payment). Entertainment and activities are organised in July and August.

You might like to know

Four signposted nature walks are a great way of discovering the natural surroundings of Turnhout. One of the longest and most beautiful walks leads through the fens.

- ✔ Environmental accreditation
- ✔ Reduced energy/water consumption policy
- ✔ Recycling and reusing policy
- ✔ Information about walking and cycling
- ✔ Footpaths within 500 m. of the site
- ✔ Fishing within 1 km.
- ○ Riding or pony trekking within 1 km.
- ✔ Direct river or lake access
- ○ Area of outstanding natural beauty or National Park within 10 km.
- ○ Wildlife haven (on site or within 1 km)
- ✔ Public transport
- ✔ Dogs welcome

Facilities: Three toilet blocks provide hot showers on payment (€ 0.50), some washbasins in cabins and facilities for disabled visitors. Dishwashing (hot water € 0.20). Launderette. Motorcaravan services. Shop (1/4-30/9). Café/restaurant (daily 1/4-30/9, w/ends only other times, closed 16/11-25/1). Breakfast served in high season. Club/TV room. Lake swimming. Fishing. Tennis. Boules. Volleyball. Basketball. Adventure play area. Bicycle hire. English is spoken. Overnight pitches for vehicles under 3.5 t. In low season reception opens for limited hours (14.00-17.00). WiFi throughout (free). Off site: Riding 1.5 km. Boat launching 3 km. Golf 15 km.

Open: 16 January - 15 December.

Directions: Site is northeast of Turnhout off the N119. Approaching from Antwerp on E34/A12 take Turnhout ring road to the end (not a complete ring) and turn right. There is a small site sign to right in 1.5 km. then a country lane.

GPS: 51.35757, 4.95896

Charges guide

Per unit incl. 2 persons
and electricity € 19,00 - € 25,00

dog € 1,50

Facilities: Three modern, heated toilet blocks are well equipped with some washbasins in cabins and have facilities for disabled visitors. Hairdryer. Laundry facilities. Motorcaravan services. Washing machine. Bar. Restaurant. TV room. Tennis. Play area. Multisports terrain. Pétanque. Bicycle hire. Mobile homes for rent (one adapted for disabled users). Free WiFi over site. Off site: Walking and cycling tracks. Golf. Antwerp. Bobbejaanlaand amusement park

Open: All year.

Directions: Approaching from Antwerp, head east on A21/E34 motorway as far as exit 24 (Turnhout). Leave here and head south on the N19 to Kasterlee, and then west on N123 to Lichtaart. Follow signs to the site.

GPS: 51.21136, 4.90298

Charges guide

Per unit incl. 2 persons € 13,95 - € 19,90	
extra person € 4,70	
child (3-11 yrs) € 3,30	
dog (max. 1) € 3,80	

Belgium – Lichtaart

Camping Floréal Kempen

Herentalsesteenweg 64, B-2460 Lichtaart (Antwerp)
t: 014 556 120 e: kempen@florealgroup.be
alanrogers.com/BE0665 www.florealgroup.be/page/kempen-lichtaart.html

Accommodation: ☑ Pitch ☑ Mobile home/chalet ○ Hotel/B&B ○ Apartment

This is an attractive woodland site and a member of the Floréal group. It is located close to the well known Purperen Heide, a superb nature reserve with 15 scenic footpaths leading through it. There are 228 pitches, of which only 32 are reserved for touring units. These are of a good size (100 sq.m. or more), all with 16A electricity and most with their own water supply. Two simple cabins are available for hikers, as well as fully equipped mobile homes. There are some good leisure facilities, including tennis and a multisports pitch, as well as a popular bar and restaurant. Day trips to Antwerp are very much a possibility. The old city is a gem with a great deal of interest, including over a thousand noted monuments, a diamond museum and the Rubens trail. Another popular visit is to the charming Bobbejaanlaand amusement park. There are miles of forest trails and the site's friendly managers will be pleased to recommend routes.

You might like to know

The site has two hikers' chalets for rent on a nightly basis, for those undertaking long-distance walks in the area.

☑ Environmental accreditation
☑ Reduced energy/water consumption policy
☑ Recycling and reusing policy
☑ Information about walking and cycling
☑ Footpaths within 500 m. of the site
○ Fishing within 1 km.
○ Riding or pony trekking within 1 km.
○ Direct river or lake access
☑ Area of outstanding natural beauty or National Park within 10 km.
○ Wildlife haven (on site or within 1 km)
☑ Public transport
☑ Dogs welcome

Facilities:
All the facilities that one would expect of a large site are available. Showers are free, washbasins both open and in cabins. Baby room. Laundry room with washing machines and dryers. Shop, restaurant, bar and takeaway (4/4-2/11). Heated outdoor swimming pool (1/5-1/9), paddling pool and slide. Sports field. Tennis. Bicycle hire. Playground and club for children. Entertainment programme during school holidays. Varied activity programme, including archery, canoeing, climbing, abseiling and walking. WiFi (charged). Off site: La Roche en Ardennes and Baraque de Fraiture (ski resort) 10 km. Golf 20 km.

Open: All year.

Directions: From E25/A26 autoroute (Liège-Luxembourg) take exit 50 then the N89 southwest towards La Roche. After 8 km. turn right (north) on N841 to Dochamps where site is signed.
GPS: 50.23127, 5.62583

Charges guide
Per unit incl. 2 persons
and electricity € 21,50 - € 37,50

extra person (over 4 yrs) € 3,00 - € 6,00

dog (high season max. 1) € 2,00 - € 4,00

Belgium – Dochamps

Panoramacamping Petite Suisse

Al Bounire 27, B-6960 Dochamps (Luxembourg)
t: 084 444 030   e: info@petitesuisse.be
alanrogers.com/BE0735   www.petitesuisse.be

Accommodation: ☑ Pitch   ☑ Mobile home/chalet   ○ Hotel/B&B   ○ Apartment

This quiet site is set in the picturesque countryside of the Belgian Ardennes, a region in which rivers flow through valleys bordered by vast forests where horses are still usefully employed. Set on a southerly slope, the site is mostly open and offers wide views of the surrounding countryside. The 193 touring pitches, all with 10A electricity, are either on open sloping ground or in terraced rows with hedges in between, and trees providing some separation. Gravel roads provide access around the site. To the right of the entrance barrier a large wooden building houses reception, a bar and a restaurant. Close by is an attractive, heated outdoor swimming pool with wide terraces surrounded by grass. Behind this is a large play area adjoining a small terrace. Although the site has many activities on offer, the opportunity should not be missed to explore the countryside with its hills and forests.

You might like to know
The Ardennes Rangers Programme teaches children about nature and the local area. There are many wildlife parks, caves and mines to visit in the region.

- ○ Environmental accreditation
- ○ Reduced energy/water consumption policy
- ○ Recycling and reusing policy
- ☑ Information about walking and cycling
- ☑ Footpaths within 500 m. of the site
- ☑ Fishing within 1 km.
- ○ Riding or pony trekking within 1 km.
- ○ Direct river or lake access
- ○ Area of outstanding natural beauty or National Park within 10 km.
- ○ Wildlife haven (on site or within 1 km)
- ○ Public transport
- ☑ Dogs welcome

Facilities: The good toilet facilities in the main building include free preset hot water in washbasins, showers and sinks for laundry and dishes. Washing machine and dryer. Gas supplies. Shop (1/7-31/8, bread to order). Bar (1/6-30/9). Swimming pool and paddling pool (15/6-15/9). TV. Table football. Fishing in adjacent stream (licence from reception). Internet and WiFi. Off site: Bus to Chatel stops at the gate. Bicycle hire 3 km. Riding 10 km.

Open: 1 May - 30 September.

Directions: From motorway 12/E27 (Bern-Vevey) take Châtel St Denis exit no. 2 and turn towards Les Paccots (1 km). Site is on left up the hill.

GPS: 46.52513, 6.91828

Charges guide

Per person	CHF 6,50
child (6-16 yrs)	CHF 4,50
pitch	CHF 16,50
electricity	CHF 4,50

No credit cards. Euros are accepted.

Switzerland – Châtel-Saint Denis

Camping le Bivouac

Route des Paccots 21, CH-1618 Châtel-Saint Denis (Fribourg)
t: 021 948 7849   e: info@le-bivouac.ch
alanrogers.com/CH9300   www.le-bivouac.ch

Accommodation: ☑ Pitch ○ Mobile home/chalet ○ Hotel/B&B ○ Apartment

A pleasant little site in the forested mountains above Montreux and Vevey on Lac Leman (Lake Geneva). Le Bivouac has its own small swimming pool and children's pool. Most of the places here are taken by seasonal caravans (130) interspersed with about 30 pitches for tourists. Electrical connections (10A) are available and there are five water points. Due to access difficulties, the site is not open to tourers in winter. The active can take mountain walks in the area, or set off to explore Montreux and the lake. Others will enjoy the peace and quiet of this green hideaway. M. Fivaz, the owner, speaks excellent English and is only too happy to suggest local activities.

You might like to know

There is a good selection of walks in the area, many of them fairly undemanding. It is an ideal way to explore this region, and can be made even easier by taking one of the mountain trains or cable cars.

- ☑ Environmental accreditation
- ☑ Reduced energy/water consumption policy
- ☑ Recycling and reusing policy
- ☑ Information about walking and cycling
- ☑ Footpaths within 500 m. of the site
- ☑ Fishing within 1 km.
- ○ Riding or pony trekking within 1 km.
- ○ Direct river or lake access
- ☑ Area of outstanding natural beauty or National Park within 10 km.
- ○ Wildlife haven (on site or within 1 km)
- ☑ Public transport
- ☑ Dogs welcome

Facilities: The main toilet block, heated in cool weather, is situated at the rear of the hotel and has free hot water in washbasins (in cabins) and charged for showers (CHF 1.00). A new modern toilet block has been added near the top of the site. Washing machines and dryers. Shop. Café/bar. New restaurant. Small lounge with kitchen, TV/DVD and library. Indoor pool complex with spa facilities. Physiotherapy suite. Ski facilities including a drying room. Large refurbished play area with a rafting pool fed by fresh water from the mountain stream. Dog bath. Free shuttle bus. Torches useful. WiFi (charged). Off site: Golf driving range and 18-hole course nearby. Fishing and bicycle hire 1 km. Riding 2 km. Cable car to mountain top.

Open: All year.

Directions: From N2 Gotthard motorway, leave at exit 33 Stans-Sud and follow signs to Engelberg. Turn right at T-junction on edge of town and follow signs to 'Wasserfall' and site.

GPS: 46.80940, 8.42367

Charges guide

Per person	CHF 9,00 - CHF 11,00
child (6-15 yrs)	CHF 4,50 - CHF 5,50
pitch incl. electricity (plus meter)	CHF 15,00 - CHF 17,00
dog	CHF 3,00

Switzerland – Engelberg

Camping Eienwäldli

Wasserfallstrasse 108, CH-6390 Engelberg (Unterwalden)
t: 041 637 1949   e: info@eienwaeldli.ch
alanrogers.com/CH9570   www.eienwaeldli.ch

Accommodation: ☑ Pitch ☑ Mobile home/chalet ☑ Hotel/B&B ○ Apartment

Idyllically situated near the beautiful village of Engelberg, surrounded by mountains, 3,500 feet above sea level, this all-year site must be one of the very best in Switzerland. The comprehensive range of facilities would be hard to beat. Half of the site is taken up by static caravans which are grouped together at one side. The camping area is in two parts – nearest the entrance there are 57 hardstandings for caravans and motorcaravans, all with electricity (metered), and beyond this is a flat meadow for about 70 tents. Reception can be found in the very modern foyer of the Eienwäldli Hotel which also houses the indoor pool, health complex, excellent shop and café/bar. The indoor pool has been most imaginatively rebuilt as a Felsenbad spa bath with adventure pool, steam and relaxing grottoes, Kneipp's cure, children's pool with water slides, solarium, Finnish sauna and eucalyptus steam bath (charged for) and physiotherapy.

You might like to know

A delightful walk leads across nine bridges over the spectacular River Aa. The path leads to Grafenort, from where you can catch the train back to Engelberg.

○ Environmental accreditation
○ Reduced energy/water consumption policy
☑ Recycling and reusing policy
☑ Information about walking and cycling
☑ Footpaths within 500 m. of the site
☑ Fishing within 1 km.
○ Riding or pony trekking within 1 km.
○ Direct river or lake access
☑ Area of outstanding natural beauty or National Park within 10 km.
○ Wildlife haven (on site or within 1 km)
☑ Public transport
☑ Dogs welcome

Facilities: Three sanitary units of exceptional quality are heated when necessary. The newest unit has super facilities for children and wide access for disabled visitors. Hot water is free in all washbasins (some in cabins), showers and sinks. British style WCs. Washing machines and dryers in each block, one block has a drying room, another a baby room. Gas supplies. Motorcaravan services. Small shop for basics. Bread and cakes to order daily. Recreation room with TV. Playground. Mountain bike hire. Communal fire pit. WiFi (free). Torches useful. Off site: Adventure park 100 m. Shops and restaurants 500 m. Riding 8 km. Bicycle hire 20 km.

Open: 15 May - 30 September.

Directions: Leave Martigny-Gd St Bernard road (no. 21/E27) to the right where signed Orsieres/La Fouly. Site is signed on right at end of La Fouly village. Access is fairly tight and long units should take care.
GPS: 45.93347, 7.09367

Charges guide

Per unit incl. 2 persons and electricity	CHF 28,40 - CHF 35,50
extra person	CHF 8,00
child (2-12 yrs)	CHF 4,00
dog	CHF 3,00

Switzerland – La Fouly

Camping des Glaciers

CH-1944 La Fouly (Valais)
t: 027 783 1826 e: info@camping-glaciers.ch
alanrogers.com/CH9660 www.camping-glaciers.ch

Accommodation: ☑ Pitch ☑ Mobile home/chalet ○ Hotel/B&B ○ Apartment

Camping des Glaciers is set amidst magnificent mountain scenery in a peaceful location in the beautiful Ferret Valley, almost 5,000 feet above sea level. The site offers generous pitches in an open, undulating meadow and the rest are level, individual plots of varying sizes in small clearings, between bushes and shrubs or under tall pines. Most of the 220 pitches have 10A electricity (long leads useful). M. Alain Darbellay has meticulously maintained the family's determination to keep the site unspoilt and in keeping with its mountain environment. He intends to maintain the strong family interest and friendships built up over the years. Additional land has been added to increase the number of pitches available. This is a site for those seeking relaxation in pure, fresh mountain air or boundless opportunities for mountain walking and cycling. Marked tracks bring the Grand Saint Bernard Pass and the path around Mont Blanc within range, in addition to many others.

You might like to know

There are a number of ski lifts in the vicinity, which are open in the summer to provide access to some excellent walking country.

○ Environmental accreditation
☑ Reduced energy/water consumption policy
☑ Recycling and reusing policy
☑ Information about walking and cycling
☑ Footpaths within 500 m. of the site
○ Fishing within 1 km.
○ Riding or pony trekking within 1 km.
○ Direct river or lake access
☑ Area of outstanding natural beauty or National Park within 10 km.
☑ Wildlife haven (on site or within 1 km)
○ Public transport
☑ Dogs welcome

Camping de Molignon

Route de Molignon, 163, CH-1984 Les Haudères (Valais)
t: 027 283 1240   e: info@molignon.ch
alanrogers.com/CH9670   www.molignon.ch

Accommodation: ☑ Pitch   ☑ Mobile home/chalet   ○ Hotel/B&B   ○ Apartment

Camping de Molignon, surrounded by mountains, is a peaceful haven 1,450 m. above sea level. The rushing stream at the bottom of the site and the sound of cow bells and birdsong are likely to be the only disturbing factors in summer. The 95 pitches for touring units (all with 10A electricity) are on well tended terraces leading down to the river. Six chalets are available to rent. Excellent English is spoken by the owner's son who is now running the site. He is always pleased to give information on all that is available from the campsite. The easy uphill drive from Sion in the Rhône Valley is enhanced by ancient villages and the Pyramids of Euseigne. These unusual structures, cut out by erosion from masses of morainic debris, have been saved from destruction by their unstable rocky crowns. This is essentially a place for mountain walking (guided tours available), climbing and relaxing, but there is a geological museum in Les Haudères, which has links with a British university.

You might like to know

There are over 250 km. of marked footpaths and 100 km. of mountain bike trails, all easily accessed from the site.

○ Environmental accreditation
☑ Reduced energy/water consumption policy
☑ Recycling and reusing policy
☑ Information about walking and cycling
☑ Footpaths within 500 m. of the site
○ Fishing within 1 km.
○ Riding or pony trekking within 1 km.
○ Direct river or lake access
☑ Area of outstanding natural beauty or National Park within 10 km.
○ Wildlife haven (on site or within 1 km)
○ Public transport
☑ Dogs welcome

Facilities: Two fully equipped sanitary blocks, heated in cool weather, with free hot showers. Baby room. Washing machines and dryers. Kitchen for hikers. Motorcaravan services. Gas supplies. Shop for basic supplies (15/6-15/9). Restaurant. Heated swimming pool with cover for cool weather (6x12 m). Outdoor paddling pool. Playground. Sitting room for games and reading. Guided walks, climbing, geological museum, winter skiing. Fishing. Internet corner. WiFi in parts of site (free). Off site: Tennis and hang-gliding nearby. Ski and sports gear hire 1 km. Riding 1.5 km. Bicycle hire 2.5 km. Langlauf in winter.

Open: All year.

Directions: Leave the motorway at exit 27 and follow signs southwards from Sion for the Val d'Herens through Evolène to Les Haudères where site and restaurant is signed on the right at the beginning of the village.

GPS: 46.09003, 7.50722

Charges guide

Per unit incl. 2 persons and electricity	CHF 23,40 - CHF 34,40
extra person	CHF 5,80 - CHF 7,20
child (4-16 yrs)	CHF 3,20 - CHF 4,00
dog	CHF 2,55 - CHF 3,20

Facilities: The excellent sanitary block is well maintained with free showers and hairdryers. Facilities for disabled visitors. Baby room. Washing machine and dryer. Motorcaravan services. Shop. Restaurant/bar. Play room. Bicycle hire. Fishing. Caravans and tent bungalows to rent. WiFi throughout (charged). Off site: Disentis 2 km. Indoor pool.

Open: 20 April - 23 September.

Directions: The site is 2 km. south of Disentis. From Andermatt take the Oberalppass to Disentis. In town at T-junction turn right towards Lukmanier. Site is at bottom of hill on left, past the droopy power cables. From the East, on arriving in the town, keep left onto Lukmanier Road.

GPS: 46.697, 8.85272

Charges guide

Per unit incl. 2 persons and electricity	CHF 36,30 - CHF 44,30
extra person	CHF 7,40 - CHF 9,40
child (6-15 yrs)	CHF 3,70 - CHF 4,70
dog	CHF 3,00 - CHF 5,00

Switzerland – Disentis

TCS Camping Fontanivas

Via Fontanivas 9, CH-7180 Disentis (Graubünden)
t: 081 947 4422 e: camping.disentis@tcs.ch
alanrogers.com/CH9865 www.campingtcs.ch/disentis

Accommodation: ☑ Pitch ◯ Mobile home/chalet ◯ Hotel/B&B ◯ Apartment

Nestled in the Surselva valley with superb views of the surrounding mountains, this is an attractive site with its own lake. Surrounded by tall pine trees, the site is owned by the Touring Club of Switzerland (the Swiss version of the AA) and provides 110 flat, level pitches, 81 with 13A electricity. There are plenty of opportunities for walks, nature trails and cycle rides, whilst the more adventurous can enjoy themselves canyoning, rafting, hang-gliding or mountain biking. For children, the playground is a challenging combination of water, rocks and bridges. Hardy souls can brave the fresh mountain waters of the lake. The Medelser Rhine near Disentis is known to be the richest place in gold in the country. Over the years many people have come to Switzerland to bury or hide their gold, but if you go to Disentis/Müster you have the chance of finding some! Since the 1980s, when serious prospecting began, there has been a gold rush in Disentis. Try your luck!

You might like to know

Amongst the more unusual activities in the area, you could try panning for gold or llama trekking!

◯ Environmental accreditation
☑ Reduced energy/water consumption policy
☑ Recycling and reusing policy
☑ Information about walking and cycling
☑ Footpaths within 500 m. of the site
☑ Fishing within 1 km.
☑ Riding or pony trekking within 1 km.
◯ Direct river or lake access
☑ Area of outstanding natural beauty or National Park within 10 km.
◯ Wildlife haven (on site or within 1 km)
◯ Public transport
☑ Dogs welcome

Facilities: Eight, well maintained, prefabricated sanitary blocks provide free hot showers and open style washbasins. A new block will include facilities for disabled visitors. Laundry facilities. Mini market with fruit and vegetables. Three restaurants. Bar. Beach bar. Takeaway meals. Aquapark. Sports area. Playground. Volleyball. Direct beach access. Boat hire. Communal barbecue. WiFi on part of site (free).
Off site: Walking and mountain bike trails. Bale town. Pula, Rovinj and Brijuni National Park.

Open: 27 March - 12 October.

Directions: Site is on the coast 18 km. south of Rovinj and is well signed on the Rovinj-Pula road at Bale.
GPS: 45.01986, 13.72275

Charges guide

Per unit incl. 2 persons
and electricity € 17,20 - € 34,70

extra person € 4,40 - € 8,00	
child (5-11 yrs) no charge - € 4,30	
dog € 2,60 - € 4,70	

Croatia – Rovinj

Camping San Polo & Colone

Predio Longher bb, HR-52211 Bale (Istria)
t: 052 824 338 e: reservations@camping-monperin.hr
alanrogers.com/CR6740 www.camping-monperin.hr

Accommodation: ☑ Pitch ☑ Mobile home/chalet ○ Hotel/B&B ○ Apartment

San Polo and Colone are two sister campsites with a number of shared amenities, including reception. They are located mid-way between Pula and Rovinj and have direct access to the sea. There are 800 pitches, many close to the sea, including 500 for touring, well shaded and of a good size (100-120 sq.m), most with 16A electrical connections. Sixty mobile homes and chalets are available for rent. The beach here is long and pebbly, with a degree of natural shade. At Colone, a restaurant with terrace serves delicious pizzas and other dishes prepared over a wood-fired grill. A great site, popular with families with young children and equally suitable for those seeking a relaxing beachside holiday. Bale is a delightful spot, originally built by the Romans to protect the salt pans between Pula and Porec. The town has been described as one of Istria's best-kept secrets, made up of ancient cobblestone alleyways, with a stillness and alluring magical atmosphere.

You might like to know

San Polo & Colone offers a real back-to-nature holiday in a very natural landscape, right beside this attractive coastline. The deep and scented shade of holm oaks and pine trees provides ideal protection from the sun.

○ Environmental accreditation
○ Reduced energy/water consumption policy
○ Recycling and reusing policy
☑ Information about walking and cycling
☑ Footpaths within 500 m. of the site
☑ Fishing within 1 km.
○ Riding or pony trekking within 1 km.
○ Direct river or lake access
☑ Area of outstanding natural beauty or National Park within 10 km.
☑ Wildlife haven (on site or within 1 km)
○ Public transport
☑ Dogs welcome

Holiday Park Lisci Farma

Dolni Branna 350, CZ-54362 Vrchlabi (Vychodocesky)
t: 499 421 473 e: info@liscifarma.cz
alanrogers.com/CZ4590 www.liscifarma.cz

Accommodation: ☑ Pitch ☑ Mobile home/chalet ○ Hotel/B&B ○ Apartment

This is truly an excellent site that could be in Western Europe considering its amenities, pitches and welcome. However, Lisci Farma retains a pleasant Czech atmosphere. In the winter months, when local skiing is available, snow chains are essential. The 260 pitches are fairly flat, although the terrain is slightly sloping and some pitches are terraced. There is shade and some pitches have hardstanding. The site is well equipped for the whole family with its adventure playground offering trampolines for children, archery, beach volleyball, Russian bowling and an outdoor bowling court for older youngsters. A beautiful sandy, lakeside beach is 800 m. from the entrance. The more active amongst you can do paragliding or rock climbing, with experienced people to guide you. This site is very suitable for relaxing or exploring the culture of the area.

You might like to know

After a busy day, why not relax mind and body with one of the soothing massages available on site?

○ Environmental accreditation
○ Reduced energy/water consumption policy
○ Recycling and reusing policy
☑ Information about walking and cycling
○ Footpaths within 500 m. of the site
☑ Fishing within 1 km.
○ Riding or pony trekking within 1 km.
☑ Direct river or lake access
○ Area of outstanding natural beauty or National Park within 10 km.
☑ Wildlife haven (on site or within 1 km)
☑ Public transport
☑ Dogs welcome

Facilities: Two good sanitary blocks near the entrance and another modern block next to the hotel, both include toilets, washbasins and spacious, controllable showers (on payment). Child size toilets and baby room. Toilet for disabled visitors. Sauna and massage. Launderette with sinks, hot water and a washing machine. Shop (15/6-15/9). Bar/snack bar with pool table. Games room. Swimming pool (6x12 m). Adventure style playground on grass with climbing wall. Trampolines. Tennis. Minigolf. Archery. Russian bowling. Paragliding. Rock climbing. Bicycle hire. Entertainment. Excursions to Prague. Off site: Fishing and beach 800 m. Riding 2 km. Golf 5 km.

Open: All year.

Directions: Follow road no. 14 from Liberec to Vrchlabi. At the roundabout turn towards Prague and site is 1.5 km. on the right.
GPS: 50.61036, 15.60264

Charges guide

Per unit incl. 2 persons and electricity	CZK 294 - 390
extra person	CZK 55 - 65
child (4-15 yrs)	CZK 38 - 45
dog	CZK 45 - 50

Camping Frymburk

Frymburk 184, CZ-38279 Frymburk (Jihocesky)
t: 380 735 284 e: info@campingfrymburk.cz
alanrogers.com/CZ4720 www.campingfrymburk.cz

Accommodation: ☑ Pitch ○ Mobile home/chalet ○ Hotel/B&B ○ Apartment

Facilities: Three immaculate toilet blocks with washbasins, preset showers (charged) and an en-suite bathroom with toilet, basin and shower. Facilities for disabled visitors. Launderette. Shop, restaurant and bar, takeaway (1/5-15/9). Motorcaravan services. Playground. Canoe, bicycle, pedalos, rowing boat and surfboard hire. Kidstown. Volleyball competitions. Rafting. Bus trips to Prague. Torches useful. Internet access and WiFi. Off site: Shops and restaurants in the village 900 m. from reception. Golf 7 km. Riding 15 km.

Open: 25 April - 21 September.

Directions: Take exit 114 at Passau in Germany (near Austrian border) towards Freyung in Czech Republic. Continue to Philipsreut, from there follow the no. 4 road towards Vimperk. Turn right a few kilometres after border towards Volary on no. 141 road. From Volary follow the no. 163 road to Horni Plana, Cerna and Frymburk. Site is on 163 road, right after village.

GPS: 48.655947, 14.170239

Charges guide

Per unit incl. 2 persons and electricity	CZK 460 - 810
extra person	CZK 80 - 130
child (2-11 yrs)	CZK 60 - 90
dog	CZK 50 - 60

No credit cards.

Camping Frymburk is beautifully located on the Lipno lake in southern Bohemia and is an ideal site. From this site, activities could include walking, cycling, swimming, sailing, canoeing or rowing, and afterwards you could relax in the small, cosy bar/restaurant. You could enjoy a real Czech meal in one of the restaurants in Frymburk or on site. The site has 170 level pitches on terraces (all with 6A electricity, some with hardstanding and four have private sanitary units) and from the lower terraces on the edge of the lake there are lovely views over the water to the woods on the opposite side. A ferry crosses the lake from Frymburk where one can walk or cycle in the woods. The Dutch owner, Mr Wilzing, will welcome the whole family, personally siting your caravan. Children will be entertained by 'Kidstown' and the site has a small beach.

You might like to know

Excursions from site include the UNESCO city of Cesky Krumlov, Rozmberk castle and Hluboká nad Vitavou, and Vitkuv Kámen.

○ Environmental accreditation
○ Reduced energy/water consumption policy
☑ Recycling and reusing policy
☑ Information about walking and cycling
○ Footpaths within 500 m. of the site
○ Fishing within 1 km.
○ Riding or pony trekking within 1 km.
☑ Direct river or lake access
○ Area of outstanding natural beauty or National Park within 10 km.
☑ Wildlife haven (on site or within 1 km)
☑ Public transport
☑ Dogs welcome

Facilities
Facilities: The excellent toilet block is heated in cool weather and provides some washbasins in cabins for each sex and a nicely furnished baby washroom, with WC, shower and bath. Laundry service. Motorcaravan services. Gas supplies. Restaurant (closed Mon. and Thurs). Small shop (bread to order). Small play area. Some entertainment in season. WiFi on part of site. Off site: The Rheinsteig footpath passes above the site. Touring and wine tasting in the Rhine valley.

Open: 15 March - 31 October.

Directions: Site is 8 km. northwest of Rudesheim. Direct entrance road from B42 (cars only), between Rudesheim and Lorch (2.25 m. height limit under railway bridge). Higher vehicles will find site signed on south side of Lorch via a one-way system (one-way for caravans and motorcaravans only; watch out for oncoming tractors/cars!).

GPS: 50.02146, 7.84579

Charges guide

Per unit incl. 2 persons and electricity	€ 24,00
extra person	€ 7,00
child (2-14 yrs)	€ 5,00
dog	€ 2,00

No credit cards.

Naturpark Camping Suleika

Im Bodental 2, D-65391 Lorch am Rhein (Hessen)
t: 06726 839402 e: info@suleika-camping.de
alanrogers.com/DE32250 www.suleika-camping.de

Accommodation: ☑ Pitch ☑ Mobile home/chalet ○ Hotel/B&B ○ Apartment

On a steep hillside in the Rhine-Taunus Nature Park and approached by a scenic drive along a narrow system of roads through the vineyards, this site is arranged on small terraces on the side of a wooded hill with a stream flowing through – the water supply is direct from springs. The surroundings are most attractive, with views over the vineyards to the river below. Of the 60 pitches, 35 are available for touring units. These are mostly on the lower terraces, in groups of up to four units. All have electricity (16A Europlugs) and five are fully serviced. Cars are parked away from the pitches near the entrance. The site is popular for small caravan rallies. A central block contains a very pleasant restaurant and small shop for basics (bread to order), with sanitary facilities alongside. With steep walks from most pitches to the facilities, this is probably not a site for visitors with disabilities; however, it is an attractive situation and reception staff are very friendly.

You might like to know

Walkers will appreciate the panoramic hiking trail through the steeply terraced vineyards.

- ☑ Environmental accreditation
- ☑ Reduced energy/water consumption policy
- ☑ Recycling and reusing policy
- ☑ Information about walking and cycling
- ☑ Footpaths within 500 m. of the site
- ☑ Fishing within 1 km.
- ○ Riding or pony trekking within 1 km.
- ○ Direct river or lake access
- ☑ Area of outstanding natural beauty or National Park within 10 km.
- ☑ Wildlife haven (on site or within 1 km)
- ○ Public transport
- ☑ Dogs welcome

Facilities: The sanitary buildings, which can be heated, are of a high standard with one section in the reception/shop building for the overnight pitches, and the remainder close to the longer stay places. Laundry. Bar. Restaurant with takeaway. TV area. Skittle alley. Shop (all amenities 1/3-31/10 and Xmas). Tennis. Fishing. Play area. Rallies welcome. Torches useful. WiFi in restaurant and reception areas (charged). Some breeds of dog not accepted. Off site: Boat trips on the Rhine and Mosel. Walking in the Hunsrück region. Cycle paths.

Open: All year.

Directions: Site is 28 km. south of Koblenz. From A61 Koblenz-Ludwigshafen road, take exit 43 Pfalzfeld and on to Hausbay where site is signed. If using sat nav enter Hausbayer Strasse in Pfalzfeld.

GPS: 50.10597, 7.56822

Charges guide

Per unit incl. 2 persons and electricity	€ 18,50 - € 24,50
extra person	€ 7,00
child (under 17 yrs)	€ 3,00 - € 5,00
dog no charge	- € 2,00

Germany – Pfalzfeld

Country Camping Schinderhannes

Schinderhannes 1, D-56291 Hausbay-Pfalzfeld (Rhineland Palatinate)
t: 06746 800 5440   e: info@countrycamping.de
alanrogers.com/DE32420   www.countrycamping.de

Accommodation: ☑ Pitch   ☑ Mobile home/chalet   ○ Hotel/B&B   ○ Apartment

About 30 km. south of Koblenz, between Rhine and Mosel, and an ideal base from which to visit these regions, this site is set on a south facing slope that catches the sun all day. With trees and parkland all around, it is a peaceful and picturesque setting. There are 150 permanent caravans in a separate area from 90 short stay touring pitches on hardstanding. For longer stays, an area around the lake has a further 160 numbered pitches. These are of over 100 sq.m. on grass, some with hardstanding and all with 8A electricity. You can position yourself for shade or sun. The lake is used for inflatable boats and fishing. English is spoken by the helpful reception staff. Country Camping could be a useful transit stop en route to the Black Forest, Bavaria, Austria and Switzerland, as well as a family holiday. High in the Hunsrück, Schinderhannes himself was a legendary Robin Hood-type character, whose activities were curtailed in Mainz, at the end of a rope.

You might like to know

The area has some spectacular hiking country, in particular the Baybach and Erbachklamm, where the flowing waters have carved dramatic gorges through the stone.

- ○ Environmental accreditation
- ○ Reduced energy/water consumption policy
- ○ Recycling and reusing policy
- ☑ Information about walking and cycling
- ☑ Footpaths within 500 m. of the site
- ☑ Fishing within 1 km.
- ○ Riding or pony trekking within 1 km.
- ☑ Direct river or lake access
- ○ Area of outstanding natural beauty or National Park within 10 km.
- ☑ Wildlife haven (on site or within 1 km)
- ○ Public transport
- ☑ Dogs welcome

Facilities: In the main building, facilities are of good quality with two private cabins, separate toilets, dishwashing, washing machine and dryer. Small shop for basics, beer and local wines. Torch may be useful. New room for tent guests and motorcaravan service point. Free bus and train travel in the Black Forest for guests. Off site: Natural, unheated swimming pool adjacent (June-Aug) with discount to campers. Public transport, bicycle hire, restaurants and other shops in Sulzburg 1.5 km. Riding 3 km. Fishing 8 km. Golf 12 km. Europa Park is less than an hour away.

Open: All year.

Directions: Site is easily reached from autobahn A5/E35. Take exit 64 for Bad Krozingen, south of Freiburg, onto B3 south to Heitersheim, then through Sulzburg, or if coming from south, exit 65 through Müllheim, Heitersheim and Sulzburg. Reception is to left of road. Note: arch in Sulzburg has only 3.1 m. height clearance.

GPS: 47.83548, 7.72337

Charges guide

Per unit incl. 2 persons and electricity (plus meter)	€ 19,50 - € 22,50
extra person	€ 7,00
child (1-15 yrs)	€ 4,00

Germany – Sulzburg

Terrassen-Camping Alte Sägemühle

Badstrasse 57, D-79295 Sulzburg (Baden-Württemberg)
t: 076 345 51181   e: info@camping-alte-saegemuehle.de
alanrogers.com/DE34520 www.camping-alte-saegemuehle.de

Accommodation: ☑ Pitch   ○ Mobile home/chalet   ○ Hotel/B&B   ○ Apartment

This site lies just beyond the beautiful old town of Sulzburg with its narrow streets, and is on a peaceful road leading only to a natural swimming pool (formerly the mill pond) and a small hotel. It is set in a tree-covered valley with a stream running through the centre and is divided into terraced areas, each enclosed by high hedges and trees. Electrical connections (16A) are available on 42 of the 45 large touring pitches (long leads may be necessary). The site has been kept as natural as possible and is perfect for those seeking peace and quiet. The main building by the entrance houses reception, a small shop (which stocks a good selection of local wines) and the sanitary facilities. Run by the Geuss family (Frau Geuss speaks reasonable English) the site has won awards from the state for having been kept as close to nature as possible, for example, no tarmac roads, no minigolf, no playgrounds, etc.

You might like to know

You will find a great deal to see in the area, including ancient churches, monasteries and castles, as well as wine museums, traces of Roman history and much more.

○ Environmental accreditation
☑ Reduced energy/water consumption policy
☑ Recycling and reusing policy
☑ Information about walking and cycling
☑ Footpaths within 500 m. of the site
☑ Fishing within 1 km.
○ Riding or pony trekking within 1 km.
☑ Direct river or lake access
○ Area of outstanding natural beauty or National Park within 10 km.
○ Wildlife haven (on site or within 1 km)
○ Public transport
☑ Dogs welcome

Facilities: The two main sanitary blocks are of good quality with free hot water. A third unit further into the site is due for refurbishment. Launderette. Motorcaravan services. Small shop (1/4-9/11). Gas supplies. Large, pleasant bar/restaurant at the entrance (1/4-9/11, closed Mon). Barbecue and covered sitting area. Heated indoor swimming pool (caps required) and sauna. Minigolf. Play area. Bicycle hire. Four mobile homes for hire. WiFi (charged). Off site: Bus service 200 m. Large lakes for swimming 100 m. and fishing 500 m. Riding 3.5 km. Rothenburg with its fortifications 16 km.

Open: 15 March - 15 November.

Directions: From the Romantische Strasse between Rothenburg and Bad Mergentheim, exit at Creglingen to Münster (3 km). Site is just beyond this village.
GPS: 49.43950, 10.04211

Charges guide

Per unit incl. 2 persons and electricity € 19,90 - € 22,70	
extra person € 5,50 - € 6,50	
child (3-14 yrs) € 3,50 - € 4,00	
dog € 1,00	

No credit cards.

Germany – Creglingen

Camping Romantische Strasse

Munster 67, D-97993 Creglingen-Münster (Baden-Württemberg)
t: 079 332 0289 e: camping.hausotter@web.de
alanrogers.com/DE36020 www.camping-romantische-strasse.de

Accommodation: ☑ Pitch ○ Mobile home/chalet ○ Hotel/B&B ○ Apartment

This popular tourist area can become very busy during summer, and Romantische Strasse will be greatly appreciated for its peaceful situation in a wooded valley just outside the small village of Münster. There are 100 grass touring pitches (out of 140), many level, others with a small degree of slope. They are not hedged or fenced, in order to keep the natural appearance of the woodland. All the pitches have electricity (6A), some shade, and are situated either side of a stream (fenced off from a weir at the far end of the site). Twenty-seven fully serviced pitches are on higher ground near reception. Having already built a new reception, renovated the pool, sauna, solarium and changing rooms, and made an open-air chess and boules area, the friendly, English-speaking owners are looking to further develop the area by the lake. Birdwatchers will be interested that the white-throated dipper is regularly seen here.

You might like to know

Why not make a day trip to Schillingsfürst (40 km) and take the opportunity to see the castle of the princes of Hohenlohe and spectacular Bavarian falconry shows.

○ Environmental accreditation
☑ Reduced energy/water consumption policy
☑ Recycling and reusing policy
☑ Information about walking and cycling
☑ Footpaths within 500 m. of the site
☑ Fishing within 1 km.
○ Riding or pony trekking within 1 km.
☑ Direct river or lake access
○ Area of outstanding natural beauty or National Park within 10 km.
○ Wildlife haven (on site or within 1 km)
☑ Public transport
☑ Dogs welcome

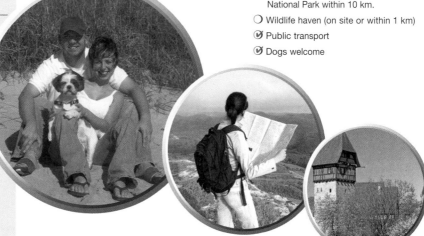

Camping & Freizeitpark LuxOase

Arnsdorfer Strasse 1, Kleinröhrsdorf, D-01900 Dresden (Saxony)
t: 035 952 56666   e: info@luxoase.de
alanrogers.com/DE38330   www.luxoase.de

Accommodation: ☑ Pitch   ○ Mobile home/chalet   ○ Hotel/B&B   ☑ Apartment

Facilities: Two excellent buildings provide modern, heated facilities with private cabins, a family room, baby room, units for disabled visitors and eight bathrooms for hire. Special facilities for children with novelty showers and washbasins. Jacuzzi. Kitchen. Gas supplies. Motorcaravan services. Shop and bar (1/3-31/12) plus restaurant (15/3-31/12). Bicycle hire. Lake swimming. Sports field. Fishing. Play area. Sauna. Train, bus and theatre tickets from reception. Internet point. WiFi throughout (charged). Minigolf. Fitness room. Regular guided bus trips to Dresden, Prague etc. Off site: Riding next door (lessons available). Public transport to Dresden 1 km. Golf 7.5 km. Nearby dinosaur park, zoo and indoor karting.

Open: All year excl. February.

Directions: Site is 17 km. northeast of Dresden. From the A4 (Dresden-Görlitz) take exit 85 (Pulnitz) and travel south towards Radeberg. Pass through Leppersdorf and site is signed to the left. Follow signs for Kleinröhrsdorf and camping. Site is 4 km. from the autobahn exit.

GPS: 51.120401, 13.980103

Charges guide

Per unit incl. 2 persons and electricity	€ 19,90 - € 26,60
extra person	€ 5,00 - € 8,00
child (3-15 yrs acc. to age)	€ 2,50 - € 4,50
dog	€ 2,50 - € 3,50

This is a well organised and quiet site located just north of Dresden with easy access from the autobahn. The site has very good facilities and is arranged on grassland beside a lake. There is access from the site to the lake through a gate. Although the site is fairly open, trees do provide shade in some areas. There are 198 large touring pitches (plus 40 seasonal in a separate area), marked by bushes or posts on generally flat or slightly sloping grass. All have 10/16A electricity and 132 have water and drainage. At the entrance is an area of hardstanding (with electricity) for late arrivals. A brand new building provides excellent sanitary facilities, a separate washing area for children with showers in a castle and washbasins in a steam river boat which blows soap bubbles in the evening. A wellness centre includes a pool and saunas, massages, a fitness room and indoor playground. You may swim, fish or use inflatables in the lake. A member of Leading Campings group.

You might like to know

The campsite organises a number of excursions, allowing you to make the most of your visit to this beautiful region.

- ○ Environmental accreditation
- ○ Reduced energy/water consumption policy
- ☑ Recycling and reusing policy
- ☑ Information about walking and cycling
- ○ Footpaths within 500 m. of the site
- ☑ Fishing within 1 km.
- ☑ Riding or pony trekking within 1 km.
- ☑ Direct river or lake access
- ○ Area of outstanding natural beauty or National Park within 10 km.
- ☑ Wildlife haven (on site or within 1 km)
- ☑ Public transport
- ☑ Dogs welcome

Facilities: One modern and one older toilet block have British style toilets, open style washbasins and controllable hot showers. Family shower rooms. Baby room. Facilities for disabled visitors. Laundry. Campers' kitchen. Motorcaravan services. Shop (bread to order). Heated swimming pool and whirlpool. Indoor play area. Playgrounds. Lake with fishing, watersports and Viking ship. Three play areas. Activities for children (high season). WiFi (charged). Off site: Golf and riding 2 km. Lion Park 8 km. Boat launching 10 km. Legoland 20 km.

Open: 4 April - 14 September.

Directions: From Vejle take the 28 road towards Billund. In Skibet turn right towards Fårup Sø, Jennum and Jelling and follow the signs to Fårup Sø.

GPS: 55.73614, 9.41777

Charges guide

Per unit incl. 2 persons and electricity	DKK 232 - 257
extra person	DKK 75
child (1-11 yrs)	DKK 45
dog	DKK 15

Denmark – Jelling

Fårup Sø Camping

Fårupvej 58, DK-7300 Jelling (Vejle)
t: 75 87 13 44 e: faarupsoecamp@firma.tele.dk
alanrogers.com/DK2048 www.faarup-soe.dk-camp.dk

Accommodation: ☑ Pitch ☑ Mobile home/chalet ○ Hotel/B&B ○ Apartment

Fårup Sø Camping is a friendly and welcoming family run site next to the beautiful Fårup Lake, a good location for visiting some of Denmark's best known attractions such as Legoland and the Lion Park. There are 250 grassy pitches, mostly on terraces (from top to bottom the height difference is 53 m). Some have beautiful views of the Fårup Lake. There are 200 pitches for touring units, all with 16A electricity, and some tent pitches without electricity. A heated swimming pool (min. 25°C), a whirlpool (free of charge) and an indoor play area for children are popular, as are the available activities, many associated with the lake. Next to the top toilet block is a barbecue area with a terrace and good views. A neighbour rents out water bikes and takes high season excursions onto the lake with a real Viking Ship which campers can join. In the last weekend of May, the site hosts the Jelling Musical Festival when the site is reserved for festival-goers, and tourers are not accepted.

You might like to know

Why not visit Legoland in the country that invented it? It is only 20 km. from the campsite.

○ Environmental accreditation
○ Reduced energy/water consumption policy
☑ Recycling and reusing policy
☑ Information about walking and cycling
○ Footpaths within 500 m. of the site
☑ Fishing within 1 km.
☑ Riding or pony trekking within 1 km.
○ Direct river or lake access
○ Area of outstanding natural beauty or National Park within 10 km.
☑ Wildlife haven (on site or within 1 km)
○ Public transport
☑ Dogs welcome

Holmens Camping

Klostervej 148, DK-8680 Ry (Århus)
t: 86 89 17 62 e: info@holmenscamping.dk
alanrogers.com/DK2080 www.holmens-camping.dk

Accommodation: ☑ Pitch ☑ Mobile home/chalet ○ Hotel/B&B ○ Apartment

A warm welcome awaits you at Holmens Camping, which lies between Silkeborg and Skanderborg in a very beautiful part of Denmark. The site is close to the waters of the Gudensø and Rye Møllesø lakes which are used for boating and canoeing, and fishing is a speciality of the site (it has its own pond). Walking and cycling are also popular activities. Holmens has 225 grass touring pitches, partly terraced and divided by young trees and shrubs. The site itself is surrounded by mature trees. Almost all the pitches have 6A electricity and vary in size between 70-100 sq.m. The lake is suitable for swimming but the site also has an attractive pool complex (charged). The pool complex is covered and comprises two circular pools linked by a bridge and a paddling pool with water canon. There are plenty of opportunities for activities including boat hire on the lake and fishing. The shop is well stocked. Both Skanderborg and Silkeborg are well worth a visit.

Facilities: One traditional and one modern toilet block have washbasins (open and in cabins) and controllable hot showers (on payment). En-suite facilities with toilet, basin, shower. Baby room. Excellent facilities for disabled visitors. Laundry. Campers' kitchen. Small shop. Covered pool with jet stream and paddling pool with water canon. Wellness facilities (charged). Pool bar. Extensive games room. Playground. Pétanque. Pony rides. Minigolf. Fishing. Bicycle hire. Boat rental. Some activities incur a charge. WiFi (charged). Off site: Riding 2 km. Golf 14 km.

Open: 1 April - 30 September.

Directions: Going north on E45, take exit 52 at Skanderborg turning west on 445 road towards Ry. In Ry follow the site signs.
GPS: 56.07607, 9.76549

Charges guide

Per person	DKK 69 - 79
child (3-11 yrs)	DKK 38 - 44
pitch	DKK 26
electricity (6A)	DKK 29 - 38

You might like to know

Canoes can be hired and a trip along the river makes a day out with a difference.

○ Environmental accreditation
○ Reduced energy/water consumption policy
☑ Recycling and reusing policy
☑ Information about walking and cycling
☑ Footpaths within 500 m. of the site
☑ Fishing within 1 km.
○ Riding or pony trekking within 1 km.
☑ Direct river or lake access
○ Area of outstanding natural beauty or National Park within 10 km.
☑ Wildlife haven (on site or within 1 km)
○ Public transport
☑ Dogs welcome

Camping Vell Empordá

Ctra Roses-Jonquera s/n, E-17780 Garriguella (Girona)
t: 972 530 200   e: vellemporda@vellemporda.com
alanrogers.com/ES80140   www.vellemporda.com

Accommodation: ⬤ Pitch   ⬤ Mobile home/chalet   ○ Hotel/B&B   ○ Apartment

Camping Vell Empordá is a friendly, family site close to the resort of Roses on the northern Costa Brava and on the outskirts of the small town of Garriguella. There are 210 touring pitches, all with 6A or 10A (extra) electricity connections. Smaller pitches are available for campers with tents. Additionally, a range of fully equipped wooden chalets are for rent. The site is terraced and well shaded. On-site amenities include a good restaurant and a well stocked supermarket. There is a convivial bar with a large terrace. The swimming pool is large and attractive and has a separate children's pool adjacent. The site has both a strong Spanish presence and also a loyal European clientèle, including some British tourists, who have been visiting for many years. Close by Garriguella is a typical small Spanish town with an interesting church, Santa Eulalia de Noves. Roses, some 7 km. away, is a smart and lively resort with a wealth of shops, cafés, restaurants and entertainment.

You might like to know

A location rich in history, culture and natural beauty, where the Pyrenees meet the Mediterranean sea. The Cap de Creus natural park and the Aiguamolls de l'Empordá are highly recommended.

○ Environmental accreditation
○ Reduced energy/water consumption policy
☑ Recycling and reusing policy
○ Information about walking and cycling
☑ Footpaths within 500 m. of the site
○ Fishing within 1 km.
○ Riding or pony trekking within 1 km.
○ Direct river or lake access
☑ Area of outstanding natural beauty or National Park within 10 km.
○ Wildlife haven (on site or within 1 km)
○ Public transport
☑ Dogs welcome

Facilities: Two large, clean sanitary blocks have facilities for children and disabled visitors. Laundry. Motorcaravan service point. Supermarket and bar (15/5-15/9), restaurant and takeaway (1/6-25/9). Large outdoor swimming pool (15/5-15/9). Children's pool. Play area. Multisports area. Fronton court. Bicycle hire. Free WiFi over site. Tourist information. Chalets for rent. Off site: Shops and restaurants in Garriguella and Roses. Cycle and walking tracks 50 m. Riding and golf 5 km. Fishing, beach and sailing 7 km.

Open: 1 February - 22 December.

Directions: Approaching from the west (Figueres) take eastbound N260, then C252 to Garriguella then follow signs to site.

GPS: 42.33888, 3.06726

Charges guide

Per unit incl. 2 persons and electricity € 18,35 - € 37,10

extra person € 5,10 - € 7,55

child (2-16 yrs) € 4,10 - € 6,15

dog no charge - € 5,00

Facilities: Toilet facilities include a new fully equipped block, along with new facilities for disabled visitors and babies. Pleasant room with tables and chairs for poor weather. Washing machine and dryer. Shop (July-Sept). Swimming pool (June-Sept). Bar and cafeteria style restaurant (all year) serves a good value 'menu del dia' and snacks. Play area. Fishing. WiFi in restaurant area (free). Torches necessary in the new tent area. No electric barbecues. Off site: Riding 10 km. Bicycle hire 15 km. Golf and coast at Llanes 25 km.

Open: All year.

Directions: Avin is 15 km. east of Cangas de Onis on AS114 to Panes and is best approached from this direction especially if towing. From A8 (Santander-Oviedo) km. 326 exit take N634 to Arriondas. Turn on N625 to Cangas and join AS114 (Covodonga/Panes) bypassing Cangas. Site is beyond Avin after 17 km. marker.

GPS: 43.3363, -4.94498

Charges guide

Per unit incl. 2 persons
and electricity € 21,80 - € 26,80

extra person	€ 5,50 - € 6,00
child (4-14 yrs)	€ 4,00

Spain – Avin-Onis

Camping Picos de Europa

E-33556 Avin-Onis (Asturias)
t: 985 844 070   e: adrian@picos-europa.com
alanrogers.com/ES89650   www.picos-europa.com

Accommodation: ☑ Pitch ☑ Mobile home/chalet ○ Hotel/B&B ☑ Apartment

This delightful site is, as its name suggests, an ideal spot from which to explore these dramatic limestone mountains on foot, by bicycle or on horseback. The site itself is continuously developing and the dynamic owner, Ramon, and his nephew who helps out when he is away, are both very pleasant and nothing is too much trouble. The site is in a valley beside a pleasant, fast flowing river. The 160 marked pitches are of varying sizes and have been developed in three avenues, on level grass mostly backing on to hedging, with 6A electricity. An area for tents and apartments is over a bridge past the fairly small, but pleasant, round swimming pool. Local stone has been used for the L-shaped building at the main entrance which houses reception and a very good bar/restaurant. The site can organise caving activities, and has information about the Cares Gorge along with the many energetic ways of exploring the area, including by canoe and quad-bike!

You might like to know

Potholing is available – why not try this amazing underground experience accompanied by one of the campsite staff?

○ Environmental accreditation
☑ Reduced energy/water consumption policy
☑ Recycling and reusing policy
☑ Information about walking and cycling
☑ Footpaths within 500 m. of the site
☑ Fishing within 1 km.
○ Riding or pony trekking within 1 km.
○ Direct river or lake access
○ Area of outstanding natural beauty or National Park within 10 km.
☑ Wildlife haven (on site or within 1 km)
○ Public transport
○ Dogs welcome

Facilities: A newer toilet block, heated when necessary, has free hot showers but cold water to open plan washbasins. Facilities for disabled visitors. Small baby room. An older block in the original area has similar provision. Washing machine and dryer. Bar, restaurant, takeaway and supermarket (all 1/1-31/12). Outdoor swimming pool (1/4-31/10). Indoor pool (all year). Playground. Boules. Riding. Rafting. Bicycle hire. Only gas barbecues are permitted. Torches required in some areas. WiFi (free). Off site: Fishing 100 m. Skiing in season. Canoeing nearby.

Open: All year.

Directions: Site is 2 km. from Ainsa, on the road from Ainsa to France.

GPS: 42.4352, 0.13618

Charges guide

Per unit incl. 2 persons and electricity	€ 15,60 - € 21,60
extra person	€ 4,95 - € 7,15
child (2-10 yrs)	€ 4,55 - € 6,75
dog	€ 3,35 - € 4,35

Camping Peña Montañesa

Ctra Ainsa-Francia km 2, E-22360 Labuerda (Huesca)
t: 974 500 032   e: info@penamontanesa.com
alanrogers.com/ES90600   www.penamontanesa.com

Accommodation: ✓ Pitch   ✓ Mobile home/chalet   ○ Hotel/B&B   ○ Apartment

A large site situated quite high up in the Pyrenees near the Ordesa National Park, Peña Montañesa is easily accessible from Ainsa or from France via the Bielsa Tunnel (steep sections on the French side). The site is essentially divided into three sections opening progressively throughout the season and all have shade. The 288 pitches on fairly level grass are of about 75 sq.m. and 10A electricity is available on virtually all. Grouped near the entrance are the facilities that make the site so attractive, including a fair sized outdoor pool and a glass-covered indoor pool with jacuzzi and sauna. Here too is an attractive bar/restaurant with an open fire and a terrace; a supermarket and takeaway are opposite. There is an entertainment programme for children (21/6-15/9 and Easter weekend) and twice weekly for adults in July and August. This is quite a large site which has grown very quickly and as such, it may at times be a little hard pressed, although it is very well run.

You might like to know

Quad bikes can be hired locally and are a unique and fun way to explore the beautiful local countryside.

○ Environmental accreditation
○ Reduced energy/water consumption policy
✓ Recycling and reusing policy
✓ Information about walking and cycling
✓ Footpaths within 500 m. of the site
✓ Fishing within 1 km.
○ Riding or pony trekking within 1 km.
○ Direct river or lake access
✓ Area of outstanding natural beauty or National Park within 10 km.
✓ Wildlife haven (on site or within 1 km)
○ Public transport
✓ Dogs welcome

Facilities:
Two modern sanitary blocks include facilities for disabled visitors and children. Laundry facilities. Fridge hire. Shop, bar, restaurant and takeaway (1/4-30/11). Swimming pools (1/5-25/10). Playground. Entertainment for children (high season). Pétanque. Guided tours and information about hiking, canyoning, rafting, climbing, mountain biking and caving. Bicycle hire. Library. Communal barbecue area. Undercover meeting area. WiFi in some areas (free). Off site: Footpaths 500 m. Fishing 1 km. Ainsa 6 km. Canoeing 6 km. Canyoning 20 km. Ordesa and Monte Perdido 19 km. Sierra de Guara 22 km. White water rafting 30 km. Jaca 50 km.

Open: All year.

Directions: South of the Park Nacional de Ordesa, site is 50 km. from Jaca near Ainsa. From Ainsa travel northwest on N260 toward Boltaña (near 443 km. marker) and 1 km. from Boltaña turn south toward Margudgued. Site is well signed and is 1 km. along this road.

GPS: 42.43018, 0.07882

Charges guide

Per unit incl. 2 persons and electricity	€ 35,40
extra person	€ 6,50
child (1-10 yrs)	€ 5,50
dog	€ 3,25

Spain – Boltaña

Camping Boltaña

Ctra N260 km. 442, E-22340 Boltaña (Huesca)
t: 974 502 347   e: info@campingboltana.com
alanrogers.com/ES90620   www.campingboltana.com

Accommodation: ☑ Pitch ☑ Mobile home/chalet ○ Hotel/B&B ○ Apartment

Under the innovative and charming ownership of Raquel Rodrigeuz, Camping Boltaña nestles in the Rio Ara valley, surrounded by the Pyrenees mountains. It is very pretty and thoughtfully planned to provide tranquillity and privacy. The generously sized, 220 grassy pitches (all with 10A electricity) have good shade from a variety of carefully planted trees and shrubs. A stone building houses the site's reception, a social room with computer and excellent WiFi connection and shop. Adjacent is a good restaurant, bar and takeaway with a large terrace that has views over the site to the mountains. Activities and excursions in the surrounding area can be organised at the helpful, English-speaking reception office. Camping Boltaña is very family orientated with a host of innovations introduced by Raquel, including a new play area, horse riding in summer, a massage area near the swimming pool, and concessionary rates at the nearby prestigious Barcelo Monasterio spa.

You might like to know

The campsite and its partner offer visitors the opportunity to try 'hydrospeed', the latest extreme sport – swim into the rapids with just a plate and fins.

- ○ Environmental accreditation
- ☑ Reduced energy/water consumption policy
- ☑ Recycling and reusing policy
- ☑ Information about walking and cycling
- ☑ Footpaths within 500 m. of the site
- ☑ Fishing within 1 km.
- ○ Riding or pony trekking within 1 km.
- ○ Direct river or lake access
- ☑ Area of outstanding natural beauty or National Park within 10 km.
- ☑ Wildlife haven (on site or within 1 km)
- ○ Public transport
- ☑ Dogs welcome

Facilities: Two toilet blocks, basic but clean and well kept, include toilets, washbasins and showers. Free hot water. Chemical disposal and motorcaravan service point. Covered campers' kitchen with fridge, cooking rings and oven. Washing machine. Small shop and caféteria. TV. Fishing. Bicycle hire. Off site: Golf 1 km. Riding 5 km.

Open: 1 May - 30 September.

Directions: Site is 7 km. south of Virrat on road 66. Follow signs.

GPS: 62.209817, 23.837767

Charges guide

Per unit incl. 2 persons and electricity € 22,00	
extra person € 3,50	
child € 1,50	

Finland – Virrat

Camping Lakari

Lakarintie 405, FIN-34800 Virrat (Häme)
t: 034 758 639 e: lakari@virtainmatkailu.fi
alanrogers.com/FI2830 www.virtainmatkailu.fi

Accommodation: ☑ Pitch ☑ Mobile home/chalet ○ Hotel/B&B ○ Apartment

The peace and tranquillity of the beautiful natural surroundings are the main attractions at this vast campsite (18 hectares), which is located on a narrow piece of land between two lakes. This site is a must if you want to get away from it all. There are a variety of cabins to rent, some with their own beach and jetty! Marked pitches for tents and caravans are beside the beach or in little meadows in the forest. You pick your own place. Site amenities include a café and a beach sauna. This is a spectacular landscape with deep gorges and steep lakeside cliffs. There is a nature trail from the site to the lakes of Toriseva and pleasant excursions to the Esteri Zoo and the village shop in Keskinen. The Helvetinjärvi National Park is nearby. Facilities at the site are rather basic but very clean and well kept. This is a glorious place for a nature loving tourist looking to relax.

You might like to know

The peaceful setting of this site offers visitors a truly tranquil experience.

○ Environmental accreditation
☑ Reduced energy/water consumption policy
☑ Recycling and reusing policy
☑ Information about walking and cycling
○ Footpaths within 500 m. of the site
☑ Fishing within 1 km.
○ Riding or pony trekking within 1 km.
☑ Direct river or lake access
○ Area of outstanding natural beauty or National Park within 10 km.
☑ Wildlife haven (on site or within 1 km)
○ Public transport
☑ Dogs welcome

Facilities: Sanitary facilities include toilets and showers. Laundry facilities. Campers' kitchen. Shop. Café. Bar (1/5-30/9). Restaurant. Takeaway (1/5-30/9). Direct lake access. Saunas. Fishing. Minigolf. Boat and canoe hire. Bicycle hire. Guided tours. Play area. Tourist information. Chalets for rent. Off site: Walking and cycle routes. Golf 30 km. Boat trips. Helvetinjärvi National Park.

Open: All year.

Directions: From Helsinki, head north on the E12 motorway to Tampere and then northeast on N63-9 to Orivesi. Then, continue north on route 66 to Ruovesi and follow signs to the site.

GPS: 61.99413, 24.069843

Charges guide

Per unit incl. 2 persons
and electricity € 30,00

extra person € 4,50

child (under 15 yrs) € 2,00

Finland – Ruovesi

Camping Haapasaaren Lomakylä

Haapasaarentie 5, FIN-34600 Ruovesi (Häme)
t: 044 080 0290 e: lomakyla@haapasaari.fi
alanrogers.com/FI2840 www.haapasaari.fi

Accommodation: ✔ Pitch ✔ Mobile home/chalet ✔ Hotel/B&B ○ Apartment

Haapasaaren is located on Lake Näsijärvi, around 70 km. north of Tampere in south western Finland. This is a well equipped site with a café and restaurant, a traditional Finnish outside dancing area and, of course, plenty of saunas! Rowing boats, canoes, cycles and, during the winter months, sleds are all available for rent. Fishing is very popular here. Pitches are grassy and of a good size. There is also a good range of accommodation to rent, including holiday cottages with saunas. The cosy restaurant, Jätkäinkämppä, has an attractive terrace and fine views across the lake. Alternatively, the site's café, Portinpieli, offers a range of snacks as well as Internet access. Haapasaaren's friendly owners organise a series of guided tours throughout the year. These include hiking and nature treks, berry and mushroom picking, and, during the winter, ice fishing and cross-country skiing.

You might like to know

Camping Haapasaaren is the ideal place to relax amongst nature. In fact, it is an island surrounded by shimmering blue water.

○ Environmental accreditation
✔ Reduced energy/water consumption policy
✔ Recycling and reusing policy
✔ Information about walking and cycling
✔ Footpaths within 500 m. of the site
✔ Fishing within 1 km.
○ Riding or pony trekking within 1 km.
✔ Direct river or lake access
✔ Area of outstanding natural beauty or National Park within 10 km.
✔ Wildlife haven (on site or within 1 km)
○ Public transport
✔ Dogs welcome

Facilities: Sanitary block includes toilets and showers. Laundry and campers' kitchen. Lakeside sauna (charged). Bar and restaurant. Charcoal barbecues are not permitted. Barbecue hut with logs. Small beach. Fishing and boating on lake. TV room. WiFi. Off site: Tankavaaran Kansainvalinen Kulamuseo, a gold mining experience where you can try gold panning, keeping what you find! The Northern Lapland Centre and the Sami Museum, displaying cultural and natural history exhibitions.

Open: 15 May - 15 September.

Directions: Ukonjärvi Camping is 11 km. north of Ivalo on road 4. Look for signs to Lake Inari viewpoint; site is 1 km. down a narrow road (signed).

GPS: 68.73687, 27.47687

Charges guide

Per unit incl. 2 persons and electricity	€ 23,50
extra person	€ 4,00
child	€ 2,50

Finland – Ivalo

Ukonjärvi Camping

Ukonjärventi 141, FIN-99801 Ivalo (Lapland)
t: 016 667 501   e: nuttu@ukolo.fi
alanrogers.com/FI2995   www.ukolo.fi

Accommodation: ☑ Pitch   ☑ Mobile home/chalet   ○ Hotel/B&B   ○ Apartment

Ukonjärvi Camping lies on the banks of Lake Inari, situated in a forested area alongside a nature reserve. It is a quiet, peaceful site, ideal for rest and relaxation. Thirty touring pitches have electricity and are surrounded by pine and beech trees. Cottages are available to rent. A bar and restaurant are located at reception; a range of local dishes are produced including reindeer casserole. There is also a barbecue hut located in the centre of the site if you prefer to cook your own food. A climb up to the nearby viewpoint offers spectacular views over the lake – you can even see over to Russia. The lake also provides plenty of opportunities for boating and fishing.

You might like to know

This must surely be one of the few opportunities to take a holiday north of the Arctic Circle.

- ○ Environmental accreditation
- ○ Reduced energy/water consumption policy
- ○ Recycling and reusing policy
- ☑ Information about walking and cycling
- ☑ Footpaths within 500 m. of the site
- ☑ Fishing within 1 km.
- ○ Riding or pony trekking within 1 km.
- ☑ Direct river or lake access
- ☑ Area of outstanding natural beauty or National Park within 10 km.
- ○ Wildlife haven (on site or within 1 km)
- ○ Public transport
- ☑ Dogs welcome

Facilities: Toilet block includes facilities for babies and disabled visitors. Laundry room. Motorcaravan services. Shop. Small swimming pool and sunbathing area. Entertainment in high season. Weekly barbecues and welcome drinks on Sundays. Fishing. Bicycle hire. WiFi (charged). Off site: The nearest restaurant is located at the national stud for the famous Merens horses just 200 m. away and will deliver takeaway meals to your pitch. Several restaurants and shops within a few minutes drive. Golf 5 km.

Open: 1 March - 30 October.

Directions: Site is southeast of the village La Bastide-de-Sérou. Take the D15 towards Nescus and site is on right after 1 km.

GPS: 43.00182, 1.44538

Charges guide

Per unit incl. 2 persons and electricity	€ 15,50 - € 27,80
extra person	€ 4,30 - € 6,50
child (2-13 yrs)	€ 2,30 - € 4,80
dog	€ 1,20 - € 2,60

France – La Bastide-de-Sérou

Flower Camping l'Arize

Lieu-dit Bourtol, F-09240 La Bastide-de-Sérou (Ariège)
t: 05 61 65 81 51   e: mail@camping-arize.com
alanrogers.com/FR09020   www.camping-arize.com

Accommodation: ☑ Pitch   ☑ Mobile home/chalet   ○ Hotel/B&B   ○ Apartment

The site sits in a delightful, tranquil valley among the foothills of the Pyrenees and is just east of the interesting village of La Bastide-de-Sérou, beside the River Arize (good trout fishing). The river is fenced for the safety of children on the site, but may be accessed just outside the gate. The 71 large touring pitches are neatly laid out on level grass within the spacious site. All have 6/10A electricity and are mostly separated into bays by hedges and young trees. Full services are available to some pitches with access to a small toilet block. You will receive a warm welcome from Dominique and Brigitte at this friendly little family site, and Brigitte speaks excellent English. Discounts have been negotiated for several of the local attractions (details are in the comprehensive pack provided on arrival – in your own language). This is a comfortable and relaxing base for touring this beautiful part of the Pyrenees within easy reach of the medieval town of Foix and even Andorra.

You might like to know

Why not take a trip to the unique Reptile Farm, home to lizards, boas, iguanas and pythons. You can even feed the centenarian tortoises!

○ Environmental accreditation
☑ Reduced energy/water consumption policy
☑ Recycling and reusing policy
☑ Information about walking and cycling
☑ Footpaths within 500 m. of the site
☑ Fishing within 1 km.
☑ Riding or pony trekking within 1 km.
☑ Direct river or lake access
☑ Area of outstanding natural beauty or National Park within 10 km.
☑ Wildlife haven (on site or within 1 km)
○ Public transport
☑ Dogs welcome

Facilities:
Facilities: Several unisex units provide toilets and facilities for disabled visitors (by key), showers and washbasins in cabins and laundry facilities. A new block has just been added. Small shop (July/Aug). Swimming pool (12x8 m; 15/05-15/9). Paddling pool (July/Aug). Play area. Gas and electric barbecues permitted. WiFi in some areas (charged). Off site: Riding and bicycle hire 1 km. Golf and fishing 5 km. Beach 60 km. at Ste Marie-de-la-Mer.

Open: 15 March - 15 October.

Directions: Site is southeast of Graveson. From the N570 at new roundabout take D5 towards St Rémy and Maillane and site is 500 m. on left.

GPS: 43.84397, 4.78131

Charges guide

Per unit incl. 2 persons and electricity € 29,00 - € 31,00	
extra person € 5,10 - € 7,50	
child (1-10 yrs) € 3,80 - € 5,30	
dog € 2,00	

Camping les Micocouliers

445 route de Cassoulen, F-13690 Graveson-en-Provence (Bouches du Rhône)
t: 04 90 95 81 49   e: micocou@orange.fr
alanrogers.com/FR13060   www.lesmicocouliers.fr

Accommodation: ☑ Pitch ☑ Mobile home/chalet ○ Hotel/B&B ○ Apartment

M. and Mme. Riehl started work on les Micocouliers in 1997 and they have developed a comfortable site. On the outskirts of the town, the site is only some 10 km. from Saint Rémy and Avignon. Purpose built, terracotta houses in a raised position provide all the facilities at present. The 116 pitches radiate out from here with the pool and entrance to one side. The pitches are on level grass, separated by small bushes, and shade is developing well. Electricity connections are possible (4-10A). There are also a few mobile homes. The popular swimming pool is a welcome addition. Bread can be ordered and a small shop is opened in July and August. The owners are most helpful in suggesting places to eat and places to visit with suggested itineraries for tours on foot, by cycle or by car. Each village in the area offers entertainment on different days of the week so you are never short of opportunities to experience the real France.

You might like to know

Local features include the small mountains of the Alpilles and Montagnette, Roman ruins of the ancient city of Glanum, and the unique archaeological excavations at Arles.

○ Environmental accreditation
☑ Reduced energy/water consumption policy
☑ Recycling and reusing policy
☑ Information about walking and cycling
○ Footpaths within 500 m. of the site
☑ Fishing within 1 km.
☑ Riding or pony trekking within 1 km.
○ Direct river or lake access
☑ Area of outstanding natural beauty or National Park within 10 km.
○ Wildlife haven (on site or within 1 km)
○ Public transport
☑ Dogs welcome

Castel Camping les Gorges du Chambon

Eymouthiers, F-16220 Montbron (Charente)
t: 05 45 70 71 70   e: info@camping-gorgesduchambon.com
alanrogers.com/FR16020   www.camping-gorgesduchambon.com

Accommodation: ☑ Pitch   ☑ Mobile home/chalet   ○ Hotel/B&B   ○ Apartment

This is a wonderful Castel site with 28 hectares of protected natural environment to be enjoyed in the rolling Perigord Vert countryside. Of 132 pitches, the 94 for touring are extremely generous in size (150 sq.m), slightly sloping and enjoy a mixture of sunshine and shade. There are 85 with water and 10A electricity, the remaining five are fully serviced. The spaciousness is immense, with fine walks through the woodlands and around the grounds. Flora and fauna are as nature intended. Here you can feel at peace and enjoy precious moments of quiet. There has been much work done with the ecology association. The songs of the birds can be heard against the backdrop of water flowing gently down a small river on one side of the campsite. The different types of birds that can be found here are numerous. Guided walks are a feature. The site owners are friendly and very helpful and want you to enjoy your stay with them.

You might like to know

In July and August, events and nature walks are organised every week by a professional.

- ☑ Environmental accreditation
- ☑ Reduced energy/water consumption policy
- ☑ Recycling and reusing policy
- ☑ Information about walking and cycling
- ☑ Footpaths within 500 m. of the site
- ☑ Fishing within 1 km.
- ○ Riding or pony trekking within 1 km.
- ☑ Direct river or lake access
- ☑ Area of outstanding natural beauty or National Park within 10 km.
- ☑ Wildlife haven (on site or within 1 km)
- ○ Public transport
- ○ Dogs welcome

Facilities: Traditional style blocks include facilities for disabled visitors. Washing machine, dryer. Basic shop. Bar, restaurant (all season). Takeaway (all season). Outdoor swimming pool (all season, heated 1/6-13/9), children's pool (high season). Large play area. Games room, TV and library with English books. Tennis. Archery. Minigolf. Bicycle hire. Beach and canoe hire. Organised activities (July/Aug), children's club, youth disco, teenagers' corner. WiFi (charged). Dogs are not accepted. Off site: Private fishing (free) 6 km, with licence 200 m. Golf and riding 6 km. Sailing 20 km. Visits are organised to local producers and day trips (low season).

Open: 25 April - 13 September.

Directions: Leave N141 Angoulême-Limoges road at Rochefoucauld take D6 to Montbron (14 km). Continue on D6 for 4 km, turn north on D163, site is signed. After 2 km. turn right and follow lane up to site.

GPS: 45.6598, 0.557667

Charges guide

Per unit incl. 2 persons
and electricity € 20,20 - € 34,10

extra person € 4,50 - € 9,10

child (1-7 yrs) € 2,00 - € 6,90

Facilities: Two very clean traditional toilet blocks offer all the expected facilities, including facilities for disabled visitors. Further facilities are near the bar and heated outdoor pool (1/5-21/9). Motorcaravan service point. Shop, bar and takeaway (July/Aug). Football. Gym. Badminton. Boules. Tennis. Fishing. River bathing. Accompanied canoe trips, walks and mountain bike rides. Organised activities for all the family (July/Aug) but no late night discos etc. WiFi (charged). Off site: Argentat with shops and watersports centre 9 km. Riding and golf 30 km.

Open: 1 May - 21 September.

Directions: From the A20 or A89 take the exit for Tulle then the N120 to Argentat, onto the D12 towards Beaulieu. The site is on the left.

GPS: 45.0464, 1.8821

Charges guide

Per unit incl. 2 persons and electricity	€ 20,30 - € 31,80
extra person (over 2 yrs)	€ 4,30 - € 6,40
dog	€ 2,00 - € 3,50

France – Argentat

Camping le Vaurette

Monceaux-sur-Dordogne, F-19400 Argentat (Corrèze)
t: 05 55 28 09 67 e: info@vaurette.com
alanrogers.com/FR19090 www.vaurette.com

Accommodation: ☑ Pitch ☑ Mobile home/chalet ○ Hotel/B&B ○ Apartment

You are assured of a warm welcome at this immaculate site, beautifully situated beside the shallow River Dordogne and just a few kilometres from Argentat. There are 120 large, gently sloping grass pitches, 118 for touring. Separated by a large variety of beautiful trees and shrubs offering varying amounts of shade, all have 6A electricity and many have good views over the River Dordogne as the pitches nearest the river are slightly terraced. The owners run an active campsite for all the family whilst maintaining an air of tranquillity (no radios). The ancient barn at the far end of the site houses the bar and a large TV room (large screen) and the terrace overlooks the good sized and attractive, heated swimming and paddling pools. There are just two mobile homes for hire as the owner wishes to keep the feeling of a campsite. Sports facilities are very good with a resurfaced tennis court and external exercise machines. The children's play areas are also good.

You might like to know

Relaxation and peace are assured in this lush, protected valley on the River Dordogne. Sports, a heated swimming pool and children's activities in July/August are just a few of the facilities available at this family oriented site.

○ Environmental accreditation
☑ Reduced energy/water consumption policy
☑ Recycling and reusing policy
☑ Information about walking and cycling
☑ Footpaths within 500 m. of the site
☑ Fishing within 1 km.
○ Riding or pony trekking within 1 km.
☑ Direct river or lake access
○ Area of outstanding natural beauty or National Park within 10 km.
☑ Wildlife haven (on site or within 1 km)
○ Public transport
☑ Dogs welcome

Facilities: Facilities for disabled visitors. Washing machine. Small shop in reception and a small library. Swimming pool, paddling pool (from 1/5). Play area. Bouncy castle. Activity and entertainment programme. Mobile homes for rent. WiFi in reception (free). Off site: Walking and cycle tracks. Fishing 100 m. Golf, riding and bicycle hire 3 km. Binic 3 km.

Open: 5 April - 25 September.

Directions: Approaching from the south (N12) take the D786 to Binic and then the westbound D4 signed to Lantic. Site is on the left in 3 km.

GPS: 48.606365, -2.861472

Charges guide

Per unit incl. 2 persons
and electricity € 15,50 - € 20,50

extra person € 3,50 - € 4,20
child (under 10 yrs) € 2,50 - € 3,60
dog € 1,00 - € 1,50

France – Lantic

Camping les Etangs

Route de Châtelaudren, Le Pont de la Motte, F-22410 Lantic (Côtes d'Armor)
t: 0033(0)2 96 71 95 47 e: contact@campinglesetangs.com
alanrogers.com/FR22450 www.campinglesetangs.com

Accommodation: ⊘ Pitch ⊘ Mobile home/chalet ○ Hotel/B&B ○ Apartment

Les Etangs can be found 3 km. from the sandy beaches at Binic and Etables-sur-Mer. This site has 100 grassy, well shaded pitches of which around 70 are available for touring units (the rest are mainly occupied by mobile homes, many available for rent). Most pitches are equipped with electricity (6/10A). The site is hilly with coarse gravel paths. Amenities here include a swimming pool, a smaller children's pool and a modest sandy play area. A small fishing lake is located 100 m. from the site (permit required – available on site). A number of activities are organised in peak season, including communal barbecues and evening entertainment. The nearest village, Lantic, has basic services and an 18-hole golf course. Binic is a larger resort with three sandy beaches (with lifeguards in July and August) and many excellent seafood restaurants. There are some fine coastal footpaths and the site owners will be pleased to recommend routes.

You might like to know

A peaceful, friendly site just 4 km. from the motorway, ideally located for discovering the best of Brittany – Le Mont St-Michel, Cap Frehel, Saint-Malo and much more.

○ Environmental accreditation
○ Reduced energy/water consumption policy
○ Recycling and reusing policy
⊘ Information about walking and cycling
⊘ Footpaths within 500 m. of the site
⊘ Fishing within 1 km.
○ Riding or pony trekking within 1 km.
⊘ Direct river or lake access
○ Area of outstanding natural beauty or National Park within 10 km.
⊘ Wildlife haven (on site or within 1 km)
○ Public transport
⊘ Dogs welcome

Facilities:
The toilet blocks are of a very high standard with good facilities for disabled visitors. Bar (all season). Restaurant and snack bar also providing takeaway food (all season). No shop, but bread can be ordered (July/Aug). Heated swimming pool. Play area. Minigolf. Canoe and bicycle hire. New outdoor gym equipment. Paintball. Quad bikes. Canoe trips. Entertainment, sporting tournaments and children's club all in high season. Online newspaper printouts available from reception. Free WiFi in bar/reception area. Off site: Shops in the nearby village of Groléjac 550 m. Hypermarkets of Sarlat or Gourdon are not far away. Saturday market in Sarlat. Riding 6 km. Golf 20 km.

Open: 27 April - 14 September.

Directions: In centre of village of Groléjac on main D704 road. Site signed through a gravel parking area on west side of road. Drive through this area and follow road around to T-junction. Turn right, under railway bridge, and immediately left (site signed). Site is along this road on left.

GPS: 44.81593, 1.29086

Charges guide

Per unit incl. 2 persons and electricity	€ 18,60 - € 29,50
extra person (over 2 yrs)	€ 5,60 - € 7,50
dog	€ 3,00

France – Groléjac

Camping Caravaning les Granges

F-24250 Groléjac (Dordogne)
t: 05 53 28 11 15 e: contact@lesgranges-fr.com
alanrogers.com/FR24020 www.lesgranges-fr.com

Accommodation: ☑ Pitch ☑ Mobile home/chalet ○ Hotel/B&B ○ Apartment

Situated only 500 metres from the village of Groléjac, les Granges is a lively and well maintained campsite set on sloping ground in woodland. There are 188 pitches, of which 100 are available for touring units. The pitches are marked and numbered on level terraces, some shaded by mature trees and shrubs whilst others are sunny. Outside high season, you can choose your pitch when checking in at reception. All pitches have electricity (6A) and water either on the pitch or close by. The site has a good sized swimming pool and a large shallow pool for children. A bridge connects these to a fun pool with water slides. Around 88 pitches are used by tour operators. Outdoor gym equipment, paintball and quad biking are all new additions to the wide range of activities on offer at the site. A weekly excursion takes the more adventurous to the River Dordogne for a 20 km. canoeing trip.

You might like to know

Close to the River Dordogne, a network of cycle routes allows you to discover the rich heritage of some of the major tourist sites: Lascaux, Rocamadour, Domme, la Roque Gageac...

- ○ Environmental accreditation
- ☑ Reduced energy/water consumption policy
- ☑ Recycling and reusing policy
- ○ Information about walking and cycling
- ○ Footpaths within 500 m. of the site
- ☑ Fishing within 1 km.
- ○ Riding or pony trekking within 1 km.
- ○ Direct river or lake access
- ○ Area of outstanding natural beauty or National Park within 10 km.
- ○ Wildlife haven (on site or within 1 km)
- ○ Public transport
- ☑ Dogs welcome

Facilities: High quality, well equipped, heated toilet blocks are kept very clean. Well stocked shop (with gas). Good restaurant, takeaway. Good pool complex heated in low season, paddling pool. Play area. Tennis. BMX track. Multisports court. Canoe hire. Fishing. Bicycle hire. Quad bike and horse riding excursions. WiFi throughout. Large units accepted by arrangement. Mobile homes to rent (no smoking) including one for visitors with disabilities (no dogs permitted). Off site: Riding 8 km.

Open: 1 April - 20 October.

Directions: Site is 12 km. north of Les Eyzies and 3 km. south of St Léon-sur-Vézère, on the east side of the D706.

GPS: 45.00207, 1.0711

Charges guide

Per unit incl. 2 persons and electricity € 22,50 - € 32,60	
extra person € 5,75 - € 7,90	
child (3-12 yrs) € 4,75 - € 6,80	
dog € 2,50	

France – Montignac

Camping le Paradis

La Rebeyrolle, F-24290 Saint Léon-sur-Vézère (Dordogne)
t: 05 53 50 72 64 e: le-paradis@perigord.com
alanrogers.com/FR24060 www.le-paradis.fr

Accommodation: ☑ Pitch ☑ Mobile home/chalet ○ Hotel/B&B ○ Apartment

Le Paradis is an excellent, very well maintained riverside site, halfway between Les Eyzies and Montignac. The site is landscaped with a variety of mature shrubs and trees. The gardens are beautiful, which gives a wonderful sense of tranquillity. It is very easy to relax on this ecologically friendly site. Systems of reed filters enhance the efficient natural drainage. This is a family run site and you are guaranteed a warm and friendly welcome. There are 200 good sized pitches, with 45 with mobile homes to rent. The 134 touring pitches are level and with easy access, all with 10A electricity, water and drainage. There are some special pitches for motorcaravans. An excellent restaurant offers a good menu, reasonably priced and using fresh local produce where appropriate. The terraced area outside makes for a convivial family atmosphere. There are many sport and leisure activities.

You might like to know

The owners, Ellen and Ge, have carefully selected some colleagues who organise activities such as quad biking from the campsite.

○ Environmental accreditation
☑ Reduced energy/water consumption policy
☑ Recycling and reusing policy
☑ Information about walking and cycling
○ Footpaths within 500 m. of the site
○ Fishing within 1 km.
☑ Riding or pony trekking within 1 km.
☑ Direct river or lake access
○ Area of outstanding natural beauty or National Park within 10 km.
☑ Wildlife haven (on site or within 1 km)
○ Public transport
☑ Dogs welcome

Facilities: Toilet facilities are in three modern unisex blocks. One has been completely renovated to a high standard with heating and family shower rooms. Washing machines and dryer. Motorcaravan service point. Well stocked shop, pleasant bar with TV and attractive, newly refurbished restaurant with local menus and a pleasant terrace (all 7/5-14/9). Picnics available to order. Very impressive heated main pool, new covered pool, paddling pool, spa pool and two slides. Tennis. Minigolf. Three play areas. Fishing. Canoe and kayak hire. Bicycle hire. Currency exchange. Small library. WiFi throughout (charged). Activities and social events (high season). Max. 2 dogs. Off site: Golf 1 km. Riding 5 km. Many attractions of the Dordogne are within easy reach.

Open: 11 April - 29 September.

Directions: Site is 6 km. south of Sarlat. From A20 take exit 55 (Souillac) towards Sarlat. Follow the D703 to Carsac and on to Montfort. After Montfort castle site is signed on left. Continue for 2 km. down to the river and site.

GPS: 44.825, 1.25388

Charges guide

Per unit incl. 2 persons and electricity	€ 22,00 - € 39,00
incl. full services	€ 25,50 - € 46,50
extra person	€ 5,20 - € 8,20
child (2-8 yrs)	€ 3,10 - € 4,90
dog (max. 2)	€ 2,60 - € 3,60

France – Sarlat-la-Canéda

Domaine de Soleil Plage

Caudon par Montfort, Vitrac, F-24200 Sarlat-la-Canéda (Dordogne)
t: 05 53 28 33 33   e: info@soleilplage.fr
alanrogers.com/FR24090   www.soleilplage.fr

Accommodation: ☑ Pitch   ☑ Mobile home/chalet   ○ Hotel/B&B   ○ Apartment

This site is in one of the most attractive sections of the Dordogne valley, with a riverside location. There are 218 pitches, in three sections, with 119 for touring units. Additionally, there are 52 recently purchased mobile homes and 27 fully renovated chalets for rent. The site offers river swimming from a sizeable sandy bank or there is a very impressive heated pool complex. A covered, heated pool has been added. All pitches are bound by hedges and are of adequate size, 79 with 16A electricity, 45 also have water and a drain. Most pitches have some shade. If you like a holiday with lots going on, you will enjoy this site. Various activities are organised during high season including walks and sports tournaments, and daily canoe hire is available from the site. Once a week in July and August there is a 'soirée' (charged for) usually involving a barbecue or paella, with a band and some free wine – and lots of atmosphere! The site is busy and reservation is advisable.

You might like to know

There are numerous caves and castles to explore nearby, including Sarlat (2 km), and Domme (5 km), with original ramparts and gateways.

○ Environmental accreditation
☑ Reduced energy/water consumption policy
☑ Recycling and reusing policy
☑ Information about walking and cycling
☑ Footpaths within 500 m. of the site
☑ Fishing within 1 km.
○ Riding or pony trekking within 1 km.
☑ Direct river or lake access
☑ Area of outstanding natural beauty or National Park within 10 km.
☑ Wildlife haven (on site or within 1 km)
○ Public transport
☑ Dogs welcome

Camping les Valades

Les Valades, F-24220 Coux-et-Bigaroque (Dordogne)
t: 05 53 29 14 27 e: info@lesvalades.com
alanrogers.com/FR24420 www.lesvalades.com

Accommodation: ☑ Pitch ☑ Mobile home/chalet ◯ Hotel/B&B ◯ Apartment

Sometimes we come across small but beautifully kept campsites which seem to have been a well kept secret, and les Valades certainly fits the bill. Set on a hillside overlooking lovely countryside between the Dordogne and Vézère rivers, each pitch is surrounded by a variety of flowers, shrubs and trees. The 85 pitches are flat and grassy, mostly on terraces, all with 10A electricity and most with individual water and drainage as well. Ten very large pitches (over 300 sq.m) are available for weekly hire, each having a private sanitary unit, dishwashing, fridge and barbecue. At the bottom of the hill, away from the main area, is a swimming pool and a good sized lake for carp fishing, swimming and canoeing (free canoes). Two new luxury tents overlooking the lake are available for rent. From the moment you arrive you can see that the new owners take enormous pride in the appearance of their campsite and there is an abundance of well tended flowers and shrubs everywhere.

Facilities: Two clean modern toilet blocks, one with family shower rooms. Facilities for disabled visitors. Washing machine. Shop (01/06-30/09), bar and restaurant (01/06-30/09), takeaway (01/06-30/09) and a terrace overlooking the valley. Outdoor heated swimming pool with sun terrace and paddling pool (15/5-30/9). Play area near the lake and pool. Fishing. Canoeing. WiFi throughout (part free, part charged). Off site: Small shop, bar, restaurant in Coux-et-Bigaroque 5 km. Supermarkets at Siorac-en-Périgord (6 km) and Le Bugue (10 km). Riding and bicycle hire 5 km. Golf 6 km.

Open: 5 April - 30 September.

Directions: Site is signed down a turning on west side of D703 Le Bugue-Siorac-en-Perigord road, 3.5 km. north of village of Coux-et-Bigaroque. Turn off D703 and site is 1.5 km. along on right.
GPS: 44.86056, 0.96385

Charges guide

Per unit incl. 2 persons and electricity	€ 18,00 - € 28,00
extra person	€ 7,00
child (under 7 yrs)	€ 5,00
dog	€ 4,00

You might like to know

The Dordogne and Vézère rivers are 5 km. away and in the local area you can visit castles, caves, fortified villages, prehistoric shelters and much more.

- ◯ Environmental accreditation
- ☑ Reduced energy/water consumption policy
- ☑ Recycling and reusing policy
- ☑ Information about walking and cycling
- ☑ Footpaths within 500 m. of the site
- ☑ Fishing within 1 km.
- ◯ Riding or pony trekking within 1 km.
- ☑ Direct river or lake access
- ◯ Area of outstanding natural beauty or National Park within 10 km.
- ☑ Wildlife haven (on site or within 1 km)
- ◯ Public transport
- ☑ Dogs welcome

Camping Beau Rivage

Gaillardou, F-24250 La Roque Gageac (Dordogne)
t: 05 53 28 32 05 e: camping.beau.rivage@wanadoo.fr
alanrogers.com/FR24800 www.beaurivagedordogne.com

Accommodation: ☑ Pitch ☑ Mobile home/chalet ○ Hotel/B&B ○ Apartment

Facilities: Two toilet blocks include facilities for babies and disabled visitors. Washing machines. Shop, bar, restaurant and takeaway (all July/Aug). Heated swimming and paddling pools. Play area. Pétanque. Tennis. Canoeing. Fishing. WiFi in bar area. Electric barbecues are not permitted. Max. 2 dogs. Off site: Bicycle hire 2 km. Golf 3 km. Riding 5 km. Historic towns and villages with châteaux and museums.

Open: 26 April - 13 September.

Directions: From Sarlat, take the D46 to Vitrac and then D703 towards La Roque Gageac. Site is on the left, well signed.

GPS: 44.81621, 1.21488

Charges guide

Per unit incl. 2 persons	€ 13,50 - € 24,00
extra person	€ 3,30 - € 5,60
electricity	€ 3,80

Beau Rivage has a fine location, just 7 km. from Sarlat, close to La Roque Gageac, with its ancient, honey-coloured houses, sheer rock face and Dordogne river frontage. There are 199 level or slightly sloping grass pitches of which 151 are for touring units with 6A electricity available to all. The pitches are of a good size, separated by shrubs and tall trees provide shade. Large units should phone ahead to check availability. The site has a good range of amenities including a swimming pool, a restaurant, a well stocked shop and a bar. Canoeing is very popular on the River Dordogne and there is direct access to the river and a small beach. Beau Rivage is popular with families and couples as it has something for everyone. In high season, a programme of entertainment is provided including sporting competitions. There are many small shops in La Roque Gageac, together with restaurants where you can sample the gastronomy of the area.

You might like to know

Explore the rich and varied landscapes with an enriching trip to La Roque Gageac, Domme, Sarlat, Les Eyzies. There is pony trekking and a golf course within 5 km.

○ Environmental accreditation
☑ Reduced energy/water consumption policy
☑ Recycling and reusing policy
☑ Information about walking and cycling
☑ Footpaths within 500 m. of the site
☑ Fishing within 1 km.
○ Riding or pony trekking within 1 km.
☑ Direct river or lake access
☑ Area of outstanding natural beauty or National Park within 10 km.
○ Wildlife haven (on site or within 1 km)
○ Public transport
☑ Dogs welcome

Facilities:
Facilities: Shop and bar (all season), snack bar and takeaway (1/6-30/9). Outdoor swimming pool (all season). Swimming lake. Fishing lake. Play area. Bicycle hire. Activity and entertainment programme. Tourist information. WiFi.
Off site: Walking and cycle trails. Canoeing. Riding 10 km. Golf 15 km.

Open: 19 April - 27 September.

Directions: From Bergerac head east, D660 to Couze, then head south (still on D660) towards Beaumont-du-Périgord for 6 km. Turn right, C3 and follow signs to the site.

GPS: 44.78596, 0.7554

Charges guide

Contact the site for details.

Camping Village le Moulin de Surier

Le Surier, F-24440 Beaumont du Périgord (Dordogne)
t: 05 53 24 91 98   e: contact@lemoulindesurier.com
alanrogers.com/FR24950 www.lemoulindesurier.com

Accommodation: ○ Pitch ☑ Mobile home/chalet ○ Hotel/B&B ○ Apartment

Le Moulin de Surier is a very spacious and peaceful site located on the site of a former water mill, midway between Bergerac and Sarlat, and is close to Beaumont-du-Périgord, a delightful, 13th-century, fortified village. Please note that this is a camping village with accommodation to rent (47 attractive wooden chalets and mobile homes). There are no touring pitches here. The chalets and mobile homes are all fully equipped and occupy large shady pitches. Some are on high terraces and others are on a level area adjacent to a lake with its own sandy beach. The lake is used for swimming and fishing, and canoes and pedaloes are available. Leisure amenities include a swimming pool, a play area and a small animal park. Various activities and entertainment are organised in high season including karaoke, discos and a children's club. The bar, takeaway and shop all function throughout the high season.

You might like to know

Surrounded by vineyards, castles and fortified towns, le Moulin de Surier, with its tranquil family atmosphere, is a stone's throw from the 13th-century fortified village of Beaumont-du-Perigord.

- ☑ Environmental accreditation
- ☑ Reduced energy/water consumption policy
- ☑ Recycling and reusing policy
- ☑ Information about walking and cycling
- ☑ Footpaths within 500 m. of the site
- ☑ Fishing within 1 km.
- ○ Riding or pony trekking within 1 km.
- ☑ Direct river or lake access
- ☑ Area of outstanding natural beauty or National Park within 10 km.
- ☑ Wildlife haven (on site or within 1 km)
- ☑ Public transport
- ☑ Dogs welcome

Facilities: Four small, unheated toilet blocks have showers and washbasins in cubicles. One has facilities for disabled visitors, another has a laundry facility. Motorcaravan services. Heated swimming and paddling pools (15/5-15/9). Bar and restaurant (1/6-15/9). Fenced play area. Adult open-air exercise area. Evening entertainment (4/7-30/8). Bicycles and barbecues for hire. Satellite TV. Internet access. WiFi throughout (charged). Off site: Cycling and walking trails. Riding and golf 5 km. Giverny 20 km. Rouen 40 km.

Open: 15 March - 15 November.

Directions: Les Andelys is 40 km. southeast of Rouen. From the town centre, continue on the D125 and follow signs until roundabout by bridge where second exit leads directly into site.

GPS: 49.23564, 1.40005

Charges guide

Per unit incl. 2 persons
and electricity € 22,00 - € 26,00

extra person € 6,50

child (under 7 yrs) no charge

dog € 2,50

France – Andelys

Sites et Paysages l'Ile des Trois Rois

1 rue Gilles Nicolle, F-27700 Andelys (Eure)
t: 02 32 54 23 79   e: campingtroisrois@aol.com
alanrogers.com/FR27070   www.camping-troisrois.com

Accommodation: ☑ Pitch   ☑ Mobile home/chalet   ○ Hotel/B&B   ○ Apartment

One hour from Paris, on the banks of the Seine and overlooked by the impressive remains of Château Gaillard (Richard Coeur de Lion), this attractive and very spacious ten-hectare site will appeal to couples and young families. There is easy access to the 115 level, grassy touring pitches in a well landscaped setting, all with 6A electricity, although some long leads may be required. Many pitches back onto the River Seine where you can watch the barges, and most have views of the château. Of the 80 mobile homes, there are seven for rent, leaving lots of space to enjoy the surroundings, including the large lake full of perch and bream for those eager fishermen. Others can try their luck in the Seine. A nearby station will whisk you to Paris for the day, while a short drive will bring the delights of Monet's house and garden. Walk along the banks of the Seine and watch the huge passenger boats cruising there, or stroll into the main town for shopping and restaurants.

You might like to know

A verdant oasis of calm, nestling between the River Seine and a private lake at the foot of Château Gaillard. It is just 30 minutes from Rouen and an hour from Paris.

○ Environmental accreditation

☑ Reduced energy/water consumption policy

☑ Recycling and reusing policy

☑ Information about walking and cycling

☑ Footpaths within 500 m. of the site

☑ Fishing within 1 km.

☑ Riding or pony trekking within 1 km.

☑ Direct river or lake access

☑ Area of outstanding natural beauty or National Park within 10 km.

○ Wildlife haven (on site or within 1 km)

☑ Public transport

☑ Dogs welcome

Camping Cevennes-Provence

Corbés-Thoiras, F-30140 Anduze (Gard)
t: 04 66 61 73 10 e: info@campingcp.com
alanrogers.com/FR30200 www.camping-cevennes-provence.com

Accommodation: ☑ Pitch ☑ Mobile home/chalet ○ Hotel/B&B ○ Apartment

Facilities: Ten excellent, modern, clean toilet blocks (one new for 2014). Good facilities for disabled visitors. Well stocked shop (1/4-1/10). Restaurant, takeaway, bar (19/4-15/9). Excellent play area. Tennis. Minigolf. Volleyball. River bathing and fishing. Many off-site activities arranged at reception. Internet point. Free WiFi near reception. Communal barbecue areas dotted around site. Bicycle hire. Off site: Riding 4 km. Golf 10 km. Adventure and discovery park on opposite bank of river offering many sports facilities.

Open: 20 March - 1 October.

Directions: Only viable access. From D907 Anduze, take D284 alongside the river. Site signed on right 3 km. from town. Take care on the approach – narrow lane for 100 m, then a narrow bridge, visibility good.
GPS: 44.07763, 3.96484

Charges guide

Per unit incl. 2 persons and electricity	€ 19,90 - € 30,50
extra person	€ 4,20 - € 8,20
child (2-12 yrs)	€ 2,70 - € 5,80
dog	€ 2,30 - € 3,40

You are sure of a very warm welcome at this spacious, family owned site. New arrivals are taken on a tour so that they can select a good pitch. There are 226 touring pitches on the various levels, 200 with electricity (10A). Some are on the level land close to the river and others are scattered on high terraces having privacy and fine views across the Cévennes countryside. The river is very popular for swimming and in a separate section one can enjoy the rough and tumble of small rapids. There are few on-site activities. However, the family is happy to advise visitors who wish to explore off site, perhaps negotiating a discount on their behalf. There is a special area, away from the main site, where teenagers can safely let off steam. This is easily accomplished in the 30 hectares of this natural and unusual site. The site lighting is turned off at 22.30, to encourage early nights. Young children can enjoy one of the best play areas we have seen.

You might like to know

This peaceful family site covers 30 hectares of hilly terrain, between two rivers. Enjoy direct river access and a private beach, and appreciate the natural beauty of the dramatic Gardon du Mialet canyon.

○ Environmental accreditation
☑ Reduced energy/water consumption policy
☑ Recycling and reusing policy
☑ Information about walking and cycling
☑ Footpaths within 500 m. of the site
☑ Fishing within 1 km.
○ Riding or pony trekking within 1 km.
☑ Direct river or lake access
☑ Area of outstanding natural beauty or National Park within 10 km.
☑ Wildlife haven (on site or within 1 km)
○ Public transport
☑ Dogs welcome

Facilities: Modern central toilet block with family rooms and facilities for disabled visitors (no ramps and difficult access for wheelchairs). A smaller block has separate showers, washbasins and facilities for disabled visitors. Motorcaravan service point. Small heated swimming pool with paddling area (20/4-30/9). Play area. Fishing. Canoes on lake. Communal barbecue areas (no charcoal barbecues). Max. 1 dog. Off site: Small steam train passes site. Several châteaux to visit. Many marked walks and cycle tracks. Nature reserve at the lake. Riding 10 km. Golf 15 km.

Open: 17 April - 3 November.

Directions: Rillé is 40 km. west of Tours. Leave D766 Angers-Blois road at Château la Vallière take D749 southwest. In Rillé turn west on D49. Site is on right in 2 km.

GPS: 47.44600, 0.33291

Charges guide

Per unit incl. 2 persons
and electricity € 16,10 - € 36,30

extra person € 5,50 - € 8,20	
child (2-7 yrs) € 4,50 - € 5,40	
dog € 2,60 - € 4,20	

France – Rillé

Huttopia Rillé

Lac de Rillé, F-37340 Rillé (Indre-et-Loire)
t: 02 47 24 62 97   e: rille@huttopia.com
alanrogers.com/FR37140   www.france.huttopia.com

Accommodation: ☑ Pitch   ☑ Mobile home/chalet   ○ Hotel/B&B   ○ Apartment

Huttopia Rillé is a rural site ideal for tent campers seeking a more natural, environmentally friendly, peaceful campsite close to a lake. Cars are parked outside the barrier but allowed on site to unload and load. The 133 slightly uneven and sloping pitches, 80 for touring, are scattered between the pine trees. All have 10A electricity (very long leads needed) and 24 are fully serviced. They vary in size and are numbered but not marked. This site is designed for those with tents, though small caravans and motorcaravans (special area) are accepted. Several types of accommodation for hire (cabin, hut, trailer or Canadian cabin). It is not ideal for those with walking difficulties. The site is situated in an area ideal for exploring and there are numerous marked footpaths and cycle tracks close by. The area north of the lake, in easy reach of the site, is designated a nature reserve offering excellent opportunities for birdwatching.

You might like to know

Home to the beautiful châteaux of the Loire, this area also has some lush forests rich in flora and fauna.

☑ Environmental accreditation
☑ Reduced energy/water consumption policy
☑ Recycling and reusing policy
☑ Information about walking and cycling
☑ Footpaths within 500 m. of the site
☑ Fishing within 1 km.
○ Riding or pony trekking within 1 km.
☑ Direct river or lake access
○ Area of outstanding natural beauty or National Park within 10 km.
☑ Wildlife haven (on site or within 1 km)
○ Public transport
☑ Dogs welcome

Credits: R.Etienne; Huttopia

Kawan Village le Coin Tranquille

6 chemin des Vignes, F-38490 Les Abrets (Isère)
t: 04 76 32 13 48 e: contact@coin-tranquille.com
alanrogers.com/FR38010 www.coin-tranquille.com

Accommodation: ☑ Pitch ☑ Mobile home/chalet ○ Hotel/B&B ○ Apartment

Le Coin Tranquille is well placed for visits to the Savoie regions and the Alps. It is an attractive, well maintained site of 192 grass pitches (178 for touring units), all with 10A electricity. They are separated by neat hedges of hydrangea, flowering shrubs and a range of trees to make a lovely environment doubly enhanced by the rural aspect and marvellous views across to the mountains. This is a popular, family run site with friendly staff, making it a wonderful base for exploring the area. Set in the Dauphiny countryside north of Grenoble, le Coin Tranquille is truly a quiet corner, especially outside school holiday times, although it is still popular with families in high season. The Chartreuse caves near Voiron are well worth a visit, as is the Monastery, and a mountain railway goes to the summit of the Chartreuse Massif. A comprehensive guide in English is given to guests on arrival detailing all the local scenic routes and places of interest.

Facilities: The central well appointed sanitary block is well kept, heated in low season. Facilities for disabled visitors. Two smaller blocks provide facilities in high season. Busy shop. Excellent restaurant. Heated swimming pool and paddling pool (1/5-30/9; no Bermuda style shorts) with sunbathing areas. Play area. TV and games in bar. Quiet reading room. Weekly entertainment for children and adults (July/Aug) including live music (not discos). Bicycle hire (limited). WiFi near reception (free). Off site: Les Abrets with shops and supermarket 2 km. Riding 6 km. Fishing 8 km. Golf 30 km.

Open: 1 April - 1 November.

Directions: Les Abrets is 70 km. southeast of Lyon at junction of D1006 (previously N6) and D1075 (previously N75). From roundabout in town take N6 towards Chambéry, turning left in just under 2 km (signed restaurant and camping). Follow signs along country lane for just over 1 km. and entrance is on right.

GPS: 45.54115, 5.60778

Charges guide

Per unit incl. 2 persons and electricity	€ 21,00 - € 37,50
extra person	€ 4,00 - € 8,00
child (2-7 yrs)	€ 2,50 - € 5,00
dog	€ 2,00

You might like to know

Every Wednesday, the friendly owners organise a guided walk.

○ Environmental accreditation
☑ Reduced energy/water consumption policy
☑ Recycling and reusing policy
☑ Information about walking and cycling
☑ Footpaths within 500 m. of the site
○ Fishing within 1 km.
○ Riding or pony trekking within 1 km.
○ Direct river or lake access
○ Area of outstanding natural beauty or National Park within 10 km.
○ Wildlife haven (on site or within 1 km)
○ Public transport
☑ Dogs welcome

Facilities: Three modern sanitary blocks include some washbasins in cabins and baby bathrooms. Laundry facilities. Facilities for disabled visitors. Motorcaravan services. Shop. Restaurant. Takeaway in bar with terrace. Pool complex. Spa centre. 7-hectare lake (fishing, bathing, canoes, pedaloes, cable-ski). 9-hole golf course. Adventure play area. Tennis. Minigolf. Boules. Roller skating/skateboarding (bring own equipment). Bicycle hire. Internet access and WiFi (charged). Off site: Riding 6 km.

Open: 2 May - 6 September.

Directions: From A71, take Lamotte-Beuvron exit (no 3) or from N20 Orléans to Vierzon turn left on to D923 towards Aubigny. After 14 km. turn right at camping sign on to D24E. Site signed in 2 km.

GPS: 47.54398, 2.19193

Charges guide

Per unit incl. 2 persons
and electricity € 20,00 - € 46,00

extra person € 7,00 - € 10,00

child (1-17 yrs acc. to age) no charge - € 9,00

dog € 5,00 - € 7,00

Reductions for low season longer stays.

Leading Camping les Alicourts

Domaine des Alicourts, F-41300 Pierrefitte-sur-Sauldre (Loir-et-Cher)
t: 02 54 88 63 34   e: info@lesalicourts.com
alanrogers.com/FR41030   www.lesalicourts.com/en

Accommodation: ☑ Pitch   ☑ Mobile home/chalet   ○ Hotel/B&B   ○ Apartment

A secluded holiday village set in the heart of the forest, with many sporting facilities and a super spa centre, Camping les Alicourts is midway between Orléans and Bourges, to the east of the A71. There are 490 pitches, 153 for touring and the remainder occupied by mobile homes and chalets. All pitches have electricity connections (6A) and good provision for water, and most are 150 sq.m. (min. 100 sq.m.). Locations vary, from wooded to more open areas, thus giving a choice of amount of shade. All facilities are open all season and the leisure amenities are exceptional. The Senseo Balnéo centre offers indoor pools, hydrotherapy, massage and spa treatments for over 18s only (some special family sessions are provided). An inviting, part-covered outdoor water complex (all season) includes two swimming pools, a pool with wave machine and a beach area, not forgetting three water slides. A member of Leading Campings group.

You might like to know

You can spend an amazing night in one of the tree houses (two to six people, no electricity or water) or in Safari or Explorer lodges for a true forest experience.

- ☑ Environmental accreditation
- ☑ Reduced energy/water consumption policy
- ☑ Recycling and reusing policy
- ○ Information about walking and cycling
- ○ Footpaths within 500 m. of the site
- ☑ Fishing within 1 km.
- ○ Riding or pony trekking within 1 km.
- ☑ Direct river or lake access
- ○ Area of outstanding natural beauty or National Park within 10 km.
- ☑ Wildlife haven (on site or within 1 km)
- ○ Public transport
- ☑ Dogs welcome

Facilities: Three modern toilet blocks with all necessary facilities including those for campers with disabilities. Washing machine, dryer. Snack bar (July/Aug). Small shop (all season). Games/TV room. Motorcaravan services. Fishing. Bicycle hire. Play area. WiFi. Mobile homes and tents for hire. Off site: Adjacent municipal swimming pool (free), tennis courts (reduced price). Many interesting old market towns and villages within easy reach. Famous equestrian centre 7 km. Chambord and other famous châteaux. Lakes for fishing.

Open: 1 April - 15 October.

Directions: Nouan-le-Fuzelier is between exits 3 and 4 on A71 autoroute, south of Orléans. Take D2020 to site at southern edge of Nouan-le-Fuzelier, opposite railway station. Well signed.

GPS: 47.533863, 2.037674

Charges guide

Per unit incl. 2 persons and electricity € 18,70 - € 23,60

extra person € 4,60 - € 6,00	
child (2-12 yrs) € 3,60 - € 4,20	
dog € 1,00	

France – Nouan-le-Fuzelier

Camping la Grande Sologne

Rue des Peupliers, F-41600 Nouan-le-Fuzelier (Loir-et-Cher)
t: 02 54 88 70 22 e: info@campingrandesologne.com
alanrogers.com/FR41180 www.campingrandesologne.com

Accommodation: ☑ Pitch ☑ Mobile home/chalet ○ Hotel/B&B ○ Apartment

The experienced owners here, who speak many languages, are working hard to raise this site to a high standard. It is in a parkland setting on the southern edge of Nouan-le-Fuzelier close to the A71 autoroute, making this an ideal spot to spend some time relaxing whilst en route north or south. It has 165 spacious, level, grass pitches with a variety of mature trees giving some shade, with 150 for touring. All have 10A electricity, but long leads may be necessary. They are marked but not delineated and access is easy for large outfits. The site is entered through a very attractive park which has some interesting sculptures and houses the excellent municipal swimming pool (free for campers) and tennis courts (reduced price for campers). The interesting village of Nouan-le-Fuzelier is only 400 m. and well worth exploring. There are nearly 3,000 lakes in this fascinating area and several interesting historical market towns and villages.

You might like to know

The Sologne area is a real paradise for walkers. Just 1 km. from the campsite, you can explore the local fauna and flora at Le Domaine des Levrys, a fantastic wooded area of 230 hectares.

☑ Environmental accreditation
☑ Reduced energy/water consumption policy
☑ Recycling and reusing policy
☑ Information about walking and cycling
○ Footpaths within 500 m. of the site
☑ Fishing within 1 km.
☑ Riding or pony trekking within 1 km.
☑ Direct river or lake access
☑ Area of outstanding natural beauty or National Park within 10 km.
☑ Wildlife haven (on site or within 1 km)
☑ Public transport
☑ Dogs welcome

Kawan Village du Deffay

B.P. 18 Le Deffay, Sainte Reine-de-Bretagne, F-44160 Pontchâteau (Loire-Atlantique)
t: 02 40 88 00 57   e: campingdudeffay@wanadoo.fr
alanrogers.com/FR44090   www.camping-le-deffay.com

Accommodation: ☑ Pitch   ☑ Mobile home/chalet   ☑ Hotel/B&B   ○ Apartment

Facilities: The main toilet block is well maintained, if a little dated, and is well equipped including washbasins in cabins, provision for disabled visitors, and a baby bathroom. Laundry facilities. Shop. Bar and small restaurant with takeaway (15/5-15/9). Heated swimming pool with sliding cover and paddling pool (all season). Play area. TV. Entertainment in season including miniclub. Fishing and pedalos on the lake. Torches useful. WiFi throughout (charged). Off site: Golf 7 km. Riding 10 km. Beach 20 km.

Open: 1 May - 30 September.

Directions: Site is signed from D33 Pontchâteau-Herbignac road near Ste Reine. Also signed from the D773 and N165-E60 (exit 13).

GPS: 47.44106, -2.15981

Charges guide

Per unit incl. 2 persons and electricity € 19,08 - € 29,38	
extra person € 3,43 - € 5,74	
child (2-12 yrs) € 2,42 - € 4,11	
dog no charge	

A family managed site, Château du Deffay is a refreshing departure from the usual formula in that it is not over organised or supervised and has no tour operator units. The 170 good sized, fairly level pitches have pleasant views and are either on open grass, on shallow terraces divided by hedges, or informally arranged in a central, slightly sloping wooded area. All have 10A electricity. The bar, restaurant and covered pool are located within the old courtyard area of the smaller château that dates from before 1400. A significant attraction of the site is the large, unfenced lake which is well stocked for fishermen and even has free pedaloes for children. The landscape is wonderfully natural and the site blends well with the rural environment of the estate, lake and farmland which surround it. Alpine type chalets overlook the lake and fit in well with the environment and the larger château (built in 1880 and now offering B&B) provides a wonderful backdrop for an evening stroll.

You might like to know

The nearby Grande Brière National Park covers almost 100,000 acres and can be explored by boat. The Guérande salt marshes, a World Heritage Site, produce 12,000 tons of salt annually.

○ Environmental accreditation
☑ Reduced energy/water consumption policy
☑ Recycling and reusing policy
☑ Information about walking and cycling
☑ Footpaths within 500 m. of the site
☑ Fishing within 1 km.
○ Riding or pony trekking within 1 km.
☑ Direct river or lake access
☑ Area of outstanding natural beauty or National Park within 10 km.
☑ Wildlife haven (on site or within 1 km)
○ Public transport
☑ Dogs welcome

Facilities: Two well appointed sanitary blocks are clean and well maintained. Facilities for disabled visitors. Washing machines and dryer. Motorcaravan service point (charged). Shop. Bar. Restaurant and takeaway (1/5-30/9). Play area. Large children's room for activities. Canoeing, kayaking and swimming from beach at the rear of the site (lifeguard July/Aug). Fishing. Bicycle hire. Free WiFi over part of site. Off site: Walking, rock climbing, caving, canyoning and shops all nearby. Riding 9 km. Cahors 30 km. Rocamadour 56 km.

Open: 19 April - 30 September.

Directions: From Cahors take D653 east to Vers, then D662 for 17 km. to Tour de Faure. Cross river and site entrance is on right by bar/restaurant. Do not approach via Saint Cirq-Lapopie (very steep, winding and narrow roads).

GPS: 44.46926, 1.68135

Charges guide

Per unit incl. 2 persons
and electricity € 21,00 - € 28,00

extra person € 6,00 - € 7,00	
child (2-7 yrs) € 3,00 - € 5,00	
dog € 2,00	

France – Saint Cirq-Lapopie

Camping de la Plage

Porte Roques, F-46330 Saint Cirq-Lapopie (Lot)
t: 05 65 30 29 51 e: camping-laplage@wanadoo.fr
alanrogers.com/FR46070 www.campingplage.com

Accommodation: ☑ Pitch ☑ Mobile home/chalet ○ Hotel/B&B ○ Apartment

You are assured of a warm welcome at Camping de la Plage from the English-speaking owners. It is situated beside the River Lot and is within walking distance of the beautiful historic village of Saint Cirq-Lapopie. It provides a good base for those who want an active holiday with many organised activities available either on site or in the immediate area. There are 120 good sized, level stony/grass pitches, 97 of which are for touring. Forty are fully serviced (6/10A electricity) and have hardstandings. They are separated by hedges and shrubs, and a variety of mature trees give good shade. The site does attract large groups of young people and can become quite lively at times. Swimming is possible in the River Lot, as are fishing and canoeing. There is a bus stop close to the site and lovely medieval towns of Cahors and Figeac are nearby. Saint Cirq-Lapopie, a member of Les Plus Beaux Villages de France, on a steep cliff, 100 m. above the river, is a very popular tourist destination.

You might like to know

Situated in the heart of the Quercy Regional Park, the site is just a few minutes on foot from the village. With its mountainous terrain and lush landscapes, this is an ideal location for long hikes or bike excursions. The Lot river offers enjoyable barge cruises and entertaining adventures in the Regional Park.

- ☑ Environmental accreditation
- ☑ Reduced energy/water consumption policy
- ☑ Recycling and reusing policy
- ☑ Information about walking and cycling
- ☑ Footpaths within 500 m. of the site
- ☑ Fishing within 1 km.
- ○ Riding or pony trekking within 1 km.
- ☑ Direct river or lake access
- ☑ Area of outstanding natural beauty or National Park within 10 km.
- ☑ Wildlife haven (on site or within 1 km)
- ☑ Public transport
- ☑ Dogs welcome

Facilities:
Three modern toilet blocks with all necessary facilities including those for babies and disabled campers. Washing up sinks and laundry. Shop and épicerie. Restaurant, pizzeria and takeaway (all season). Outdoor swimming pool (22/5-27/8) and heated indoor swimming pool (2/5-15/9). Tennis. Multisports pitch. Go-karts. Minigolf. Bicycle hire. Games and TV rooms. Varied sporting and entertainment programme (10/7-25/8). Pony riding. Torch useful. WiFi over site (charged; free in reception area). Off site: Boat launching 5 km. Golf 7 km.

Open: 19 April - 15 September.

Directions: Site is well signed on the north bank of the River Loire, 100 m. north of the main D952, Saumur-Tours road, 5 km. northeast of Saumur.

GPS: 47.24731, -0.00048

Charges guide

Per unit incl. 2 persons
and electricity € 17,50 - € 38,00

with water and drainage € 19,00 - € 40,50

extra person € 6,50 - € 8,50

child (4-12 yrs) € 4,00 - € 4,50

7th night free in low season.

France – Varennes-sur-Loire

Castel Camping Domaine de la Brèche

5 impasse de la Brèche (RN152), F-49730 Varennes-sur-Loire (Maine-et-Loire)
t: 02 41 51 22 92   e: contact@domainedelabreche.com
alanrogers.com/FR49010   www.domainedelabreche.com

Accommodation: ☑ Pitch ☑ Mobile home/chalet ○ Hotel/B&B ○ Apartment

The Saint Cast family have developed Domaine de la Brèche with care and attention. The attractive site occupies a 24-hectare estate, 4 km. northeast of Saumur on the edge of the Loire behind the dykes. There are 235 spacious, level, grass pitches, with 135 for touring. Trees and bushes give some shade. All have electricity (some require long cables). Eighty have a water supply and drainage. The restaurant, bar and terrace, also open to the public, provide a social base and are popular with British visitors. The pool complex includes one with a removable cover, one outdoor, and one for toddlers. It is a good base from which to explore the famous châteaux, abbeys, wine cellars, mushroom caves and Troglodyte villages in this region. The site includes a small lake (used for fishing) and wooded area ensuring a quiet, relaxed and rural atmosphere and making Domaine de la Brèche a comfortable holiday base for couples and families.

You might like to know

The site is just 6 km. from Saumur, home to the famous Cadre Noir riding school (visits possible).

- ☑ Environmental accreditation
- ☑ Reduced energy/water consumption policy
- ☑ Recycling and reusing policy
- ☑ Information about walking and cycling
- ○ Footpaths within 500 m. of the site
- ☑ Fishing within 1 km.
- ☑ Riding or pony trekking within 1 km.
- ○ Direct river or lake access
- ○ Area of outstanding natural beauty or National Park within 10 km.
- ○ Wildlife haven (on site or within 1 km)
- ○ Public transport
- ○ Dogs welcome

Facilities: The toilet block is clean and facilities are good with washbasins in cubicles, new showers (men and women separately) and facilities for disabled visitors. Baby area. Laundry facilities. Shop, bar, terraced café and takeaway (all 21/6-31/8). Covered and heated pool, outdoor pool and paddling pool. Fitness centre. Play area with apparatus. Terraced minigolf. TV. Video games. Pony rides. Bicycle hire. Free WiFi over site. Off site: Fishing 500 m. Golf, riding 2 km. Sailing 7 km.

Open: 26 April - 13 September.

Directions: St Hilaire-St Florent is 2 km. west of Saumur. Take D751 (Gennes). Right at roundabout in St Hilaire-St Florent and on until Le Poitrineau and campsite sign, then turn left. Continue for 3 km. then turn right into site road.

GPS: 47.29382, -0.14285

Charges guide

Per unit incl. 2 persons and electricity	€ 20,00 - € 39,00
extra person	€ 4,00 - € 6,60
child (3-10 yrs)	€ 2,50 - € 3,85
dog	€ 2,00 - € 4,00

France – Saumur

Sites et Paysages de Chantepie

La Croix, Saint Hilaire-Saint Florent, F-49400 Saumur (Maine-et-Loire)
t: 02 41 67 95 34 e: info@campingchantepie.com
alanrogers.com/FR49020 www.campingchantepie.com

Accommodation: ☑ Pitch ☑ Mobile home/chalet ○ Hotel/B&B ○ Apartment

On arriving at Camping de Chantepie with its colourful, floral entrance, a friendly greeting awaits at reception, set beside a restored farmhouse. The site is owned by a charitable organisation which provides employment for local people with disabilities. Linked by gravel roads (which can be dusty), the 120 grass touring pitches are level and spacious, with some new larger ones (200 sq.m. at extra cost – state preference when booking). All pitches have electricity (16A, 10 also with water and waste water) and are separated by low hedges of flowers and trees which offer some shade. Water points are easily accessible around the site. The panoramic views over the Loire from the pitches on the terraced perimeter of the meadow are stunning and from here a footpath leads to the river valley. Leisure activities for all ages are catered for in July/August by the Chantepie Club, including wine tastings, excursions and canoeing. This is a good site for families.

You might like to know

Chantepie nestles in a protected natural environment, bordered by vineyards and with breathtaking views over the Loire Valley, a UNESCO World Heritage Site.

- ☑ Environmental accreditation
- ☑ Reduced energy/water consumption policy
- ☑ Recycling and reusing policy
- ☑ Information about walking and cycling
- ☑ Footpaths within 500 m. of the site
- ☑ Fishing within 1 km.
- ☑ Riding or pony trekking within 1 km.
- ☑ Direct river or lake access
- ☑ Area of outstanding natural beauty or National Park within 10 km.
- ☑ Wildlife haven (on site or within 1 km)
- ☑ Public transport
- ☑ Dogs welcome

Facilities: Three well maintained toilet blocks provide all the usual facilities. Laundry facilities. Baby room. Disabled visitors are well catered for. Motorcaravan services. The farmhouse houses reception, a small shop (all season) and takeaway snacks (5/7-31/8) when bar is closed. A bar/restaurant serves crêpes, salads, etc. (evenings July/Aug). Swimming pool (heated and covered) and paddling pool. Fishing. Play area. Bicycle hire. Wide variety of evening entertainment in high season. WiFi throughout (charged). Off site: Golf and riding 10 km. Sailing 25 km.

Open: 25 April - 13 September.

Directions: Brissac-Quincé is 17 km. southeast of Angers on D748 towards Poitiers. Do not enter the town but turn north on D55 (site signed) towards St Mathurin.

GPS: 47.3611, -0.4353

Charges guide

Per unit incl. 2 persons
and electricity € 19,00 - € 35,00

extra person € 4,00 - € 6,00

child (3-10 yrs) € 2,50 - € 3,85

dog € 2,00 - € 4,00

Sites et Paysages de l'Etang

Route de Saint Mathurin, F-49320 Brissac-Quincé (Maine-et-Loire)
t: 02 41 91 70 61 e: info@campingetang.com
alanrogers.com/FR49040 www.campingetang.com

Accommodation: ☑ Pitch ☑ Mobile home/chalet ○ Hotel/B&B ○ Apartment

At Camping de l'Etang many of the 125 level touring pitches have pleasant views across the countryside. Separated and numbered, some have a little shade and all have electricity (10A) with water and drainage nearby; 21 are fully serviced. A small bridge crosses the River Aubance which runs through the site (well fenced) and there are two lakes where fisherman can enjoy free fishing. The site has its own vineyard and the wine produced can be purchased on the campsite. The adjacent Parc de Loisirs is a paradise for young children with many activities (free for campers). These include boating, pedaloes, pony rides, miniature train, water slide, bouncy castle and swings. Originally the farm of the Château de Brissac (yet only 24 km. from the lovely town of Angers), this is an attractive campsite retaining much of its rural charm.

You might like to know

The campsite is surrounded by vineyards, cycling and walking routes and bridle paths, while the countless leafy islands and sandbanks of the Loire, the last untamed river in Europe, can be explored by boat.

☑ Environmental accreditation
☑ Reduced energy/water consumption policy
☑ Recycling and reusing policy
☑ Information about walking and cycling
☑ Footpaths within 500 m. of the site
☑ Fishing within 1 km.
☑ Riding or pony trekking within 1 km.
☑ Direct river or lake access
☑ Area of outstanding natural beauty or National Park within 10 km.
○ Wildlife haven (on site or within 1 km)
○ Public transport
☑ Dogs welcome

Kawan Village l'Isle Verte

Avenue de la Loire, F-49730 Montsoreau (Maine-et-Loire)
t: 02 41 51 76 60   e: isleverte49@orange.fr
alanrogers.com/FR49090   www.campingisleverte.com

Accommodation: ☑ Pitch   ☑ Mobile home/chalet   ○ Hotel/B&B   ○ Apartment

This friendly, natural site, with pitches overlooking the Loire, is just 200 m. from the nearest shop, bar and restaurant in Montsoreau, and is an ideal base from which to explore the western Loire area. Most of the 90 shaded, level and good sized tourist pitches are separated by low hedges but grass tends to be rather sparse during dry spells. All have electricity (16A). Excellent English is spoken in the reception and bar/restaurant. Attractions within walking distance include the château, troglodyte caves (used for traditional mushroom production) and restaurant, wine tasting in the cellars nearby, and a Sunday market in the village. Fishermen are particularly well catered for at Isle Verte, with an area to store equipment and live bait (permits are available in Saumur). Cyclists and walkers could also well be in their element here. For the less energetic, there is a bus service into Saumur with its château and other historic buildings, and all its shops, bars and restaurants.

Facilities: A modern, well maintained building provides all necessary facilities, including those for disabled campers. Baby room. Laundry facilities. Motorcaravan service point. Bar and restaurant (15/5-30/9). Heated swimming and paddling pools (15/4-30/9). Small play area. Table tennis. Bouncy castle. Trampoline. Tennis. Boules. Fishing. Organised family activities. Boat launching. WiFi (charged). Off site: Boat launching and river beach 300 m. Bicycle hire and sailing 1 km. Golf and riding 7 km. Montsoreau Château.

Open: 1 April - 12 October.

Directions: Montsoreau lies on the south bank of the River Loire, on D947 Saumur-Chinon road, 12 km. from Saumur. Site is clearly signed on western side of village.
GPS: 47.21820, 0.05265

Charges guide

Per unit incl. 2 persons and electricity	€ 19,50 - € 27,50
extra person	€ 4,00 - € 6,00
child (5-10 yrs)	€ 3,00 - € 4,00
dog	€ 2,00

You might like to know

Situated in the Anjou-Touraine nature park, the site is close to vineyards and many places of interest. Fontevraud Abbey and the pretty villages of Montsoreau, Turquant and Candes St Martin can be visited by bicycle.

- ☑ Environmental accreditation
- ☑ Reduced energy/water consumption policy
- ☑ Recycling and reusing policy
- ☑ Information about walking and cycling
- ☑ Footpaths within 500 m. of the site
- ☑ Fishing within 1 km.
- ○ Riding or pony trekking within 1 km.
- ☑ Direct river or lake access
- ☑ Area of outstanding natural beauty or National Park within 10 km.
- ☑ Wildlife haven (on site or within 1 km)
- ☑ Public transport
- ☑ Dogs welcome

Facilities: Two well kept and modern unisex toilet blocks have British style toilets, washbasins in cabins, units for disabled visitors, and two family cabins. Small laundry. Motorcaravan services. Milk, bread and takeaway snacks available (no gas). Snack bar/bar with TV and terrace (1/6-1/9). Swimming pool complex (18/5-1/9). Play areas. Bicycle hire. Pétanque. Organised activities including treasure hunts, archery, water polo and food tasting (8/7-23/8). Well stocked tourist information cabin. WiFi (charged). Off site: Riding, bicycle hire, shops and restaurants within 1 km. Beach, kayaking and Forest Adventure 10 km. Walking (routes are well signposted). Golf 20 km. Normandy landing beaches 30 km.

Open: 1 April - 15 October.

Directions: Site is just north of La Haye-du-Puits on the primary route from Cherbourg to Mont St-Michel, St Malo and Rennes. It is 24 km. south of N13 at Valognes and 29 km. north of Coutances: leave D900 at roundabout at northern end of bypass (towards town). Site signed on right.

GPS: 49.300413, -1.544775

Charges guide

Per unit incl. 2 persons and electricity € 17,00 - € 37,00	
extra person € 4,00 - € 8,00	
child (2-10 yrs) € 4,00 - € 6,00	
dog € 1,00 - € 2,00	

France – Saint Symphorien-le-Valois

Camping l'Etang des Haizes

43 rue Cauticotte, F-50250 Saint Symphorien-le-Valois (Manche)
t: 02 33 46 01 16   e: info@campingetangdeshaizes.com
alanrogers.com/FR50000   www.campingetangdeshaizes.com

Accommodation: ☑ Pitch ☑ Mobile home/chalet ○ Hotel/B&B ○ Apartment

This is an attractive and very friendly site with a swimming pool complex that has a four-lane slide, a jacuzzi and a paddling pool. L'Etang des Haizes has 160 good sized pitches, of which 100 are for touring units, on fairly level ground and all with electricity (10A Europlug). They are set in a mixture of conifers, orchard and shrubbery, with some very attractive, slightly smaller pitches overlooking the lake and 60 mobile homes inconspicuously sited. The fenced lake has a small beach with ducks and pedaloes, and offers good coarse fishing. Monsieur Laurent, the friendly owner of the site, who speaks excellent English, has recently had an outdoor fitness park installed consisting of eight different pieces of equipment all designed to exercise different parts of the body in the fresh air. This is a good area for walking and cycling and an eight kilometre round trip to experience the views from Le Mont de Doville is a must. A good sandy beach is within 10 km.

You might like to know

The campsite is accredited with the Normandy quality charter for rural cycle routes.

○ Environmental accreditation
☑ Reduced energy/water consumption policy
☑ Recycling and reusing policy
☑ Information about walking and cycling
☑ Footpaths within 500 m. of the site
☑ Fishing within 1 km.
☑ Riding or pony trekking within 1 km.
☑ Direct river or lake access
☑ Area of outstanding natural beauty or National Park within 10 km.
☑ Wildlife haven (on site or within 1 km)
☑ Public transport
☑ Dogs welcome

Camping Do Mi Si La Mi

31 rue de la Vierge, Saint Julien-Plage, F-56170 Quiberon (Morbihan)
t: 02 97 50 22 52   e: camping@domisilami.com
alanrogers.com/FR56360   www.domisilami.com

Accommodation: ☑ Pitch ☑ Mobile home/chalet ○ Hotel/B&B ○ Apartment

Occupying a five-hectare site on the Quiberon Peninsula, just 100 metres from the sandy beaches, this campsite has plenty to offer and is particularly quiet and laid back in low season. Of the 350 pitches, 189 are for touring and are set amongst high mature hedges and colourful shrubs giving plenty of shade and privacy; some have sea views. Long leads are required on a few pitches as the 10A electricty points can be shared between three or four pitches. The excellent amenities for children are in a well fenced area and include climbing frames, bouncy castles and multisports courts. Treasure hunts and other activities are organised daily in high season. The well managed reception is on the opposite side of the road to the campsite. This site is ideally situated for exploring this fascinating area.

You might like to know

The site is undergoing Ecolabel certification.

- ☑ Environmental accreditation
- ☑ Reduced energy/water consumption policy
- ☑ Recycling and reusing policy
- ☑ Information about walking and cycling
- ☑ Footpaths within 500 m. of the site
- ☑ Fishing within 1 km.
- ☑ Riding or pony trekking within 1 km.
- ○ Direct river or lake access
- ☑ Area of outstanding natural beauty or National Park within 10 km.
- ☑ Wildlife haven (on site or within 1 km)
- ○ Public transport
- ☑ Dogs welcome

Facilities: New, high quality sanitary block with hot showers. Facilities for disabled campers and young children. Separate laundry. Shop. Bar, restaurant and takeaway (1/4-15/9). TV room. Bouncy castles. Multisport courts. Bicycle hire. Children's club. WiFi throughout (charged). Off site: Bar, restaurant, supermarket 50 m. Beaches and bicycle hire 100 m. Town centre 2 km. Golf and riding 3 km.

Open: 1 April - 1 November.

Directions: From N165 Vannes-Lorient dual carriageway south of Auray, take Carnac/Ploemel exit. Continue southwest on D768 through the town of Plouharmel following signs for Quiberon. 25 km. from the N165 but before reaching Quiberon, the site is signed to the left at St Julien-Plage.
GPS: 47.49974, -3.12026

Charges guide

Per unit incl. 2 persons and electricity	€ 17,80 - € 27,80
extra person	€ 2,90 - € 5,00
child (under 7 yrs)	€ 2,10 - € 3,00
dog	€ 2,00 - € 2,50

Facilities: New heated sanitary block with family/disabled room close to entrance, but a fair distance uphill from some pitches. Washing machine and dryer. Shop, bar, restaurant and takeaway, heated outdoor pool (all season). Lake swimming. Fishing. Playgrounds. Bicycle hire. Caravan storage. American RVs not accepted. Chalets for rent with TV and DVD player. WiFi (free). Off site: Riding 3 km. Shops, bank with ATM and services 11 km.

Open: 1 April - 30 September.

Directions: St Léger-de-Fougeret is 10 km. south of Château-Chinon. From Château-Chinon, on D978, take D27 south for 3 km, then fork right on D157 for 5.5 km. to St Léger. Continue through village, follow signs to site 1 km.

GPS: 47.00587, 3.90548

Charges guide

Per unit incl. 2 persons and electricity	€ 20,50 - € 23,50
extra person	€ 6,50
child (0-16 yrs)	€ 3,00 - € 3,30
dog	€ 2,20

No credit cards.

France – Saint Léger-de-Fougeret

Sites et Paysages l'Etang de la Fougeraie

Hameau de Champs, F-58120 Saint Léger-de-Fougeret (Nièvre)
t: 03 86 85 11 85   e: info@campingfougeraie@.fr
alanrogers.com/FR58040   www.campingfougeraie.com

Accommodation: ☑ Pitch ☑ Mobile home/chalet ○ Hotel/B&B ○ Apartment

This is a quiet and peaceful, spacious campsite laid out on a hillside deep in the Parc Naturel Régional du Morvan, with views over the lake, meadows and surrounding hills. The spring water lake is ideal for fishing and swimming. There is a small bar and restaurant serving good quality regional meals and a well stocked shop with local produce. There are 73 terraced pitches, with 67 for touring, 45 with electricity (10/16A). Major renovations in 2013 include redesigned pitches with fewer steep paths, as well as a new heated, outdoor pool and heated sanitary block. Here is a place where you can sit back and relax after a day exploring the surrounding peaceful countryside lying within the Parc du Morvan. For those seeking the really quiet life there are 'introduction to fishing' courses. Fishing parties are welcome. Marked walks from the site within the forest and information on routes and local fauna is available at reception.

You might like to know

As well as walks in the forest (guides available), there are visits to farms, an equestrian farm, and the museums of Château Chinon and the Basilica of Vezelay.

○ Environmental accreditation
○ Reduced energy/water consumption policy
○ Recycling and reusing policy
☑ Information about walking and cycling
☑ Footpaths within 500 m. of the site
☑ Fishing within 1 km.
○ Riding or pony trekking within 1 km.
☑ Direct river or lake access
☑ Area of outstanding natural beauty or National Park within 10 km.
○ Wildlife haven (on site or within 1 km)
○ Public transport
☑ Dogs welcome

Facilities: Four unisex toilet blocks have showers, washbasins in cubicles, family cubicles and facilities for disabled visitors. Laundry facilities. Motorcaravan service point. Bar, entertainment area and snack bar. Play area. TV. Games room. Covered, heated pool complex including slides (5/4-15/10), jacuzzi and children's pool. Fitness room. Sauna. Multisport court. WiFi over site (free). Gas barbeques not accepted. Off site: Shops, restaurants and bars in Rue 7 km.

Open: 1 April - 1 November.

Directions: From A16 exit 24, take D32 towards and around Rue. At second roundabout take second exit on D940, then left on D4 for 1.5 km. before turning right on D204 to Le Bout des Crocs. Site is signed to the left.

GPS: 50.26895, 1.60263

Charges guide

Per unit incl. 2 persons and electricity € 20,00 - € 31,00	
extra person € 5,50 - € 6,50	
child (2-7 yrs) € 4,00 - € 5,00	
dog € 2,00	

France – Saint Quentin-en-Tourmont

Camping Le Champ Neuf

8 rue du Champ Neuf, F-80120 Saint Quentin-en-Tourmont (Somme)
t: 03 22 25 07 94 e: contact@camping-lechampneuf.com
alanrogers.com/FR80020 www.camping-lechampneuf.com

Accommodation: ⊘ Pitch ⊘ Mobile home/chalet ○ Hotel/B&B ○ Apartment

Le Champ Neuf is located in Saint Quentin-en-Tourmont, on the Bay of the Somme. It is a quiet site, 900 m. from the ornithological reserve of Marquenterre, the favourite stop for thousands of migratory birds; birdwatchers will appreciate the dawn chorus and varied species. This eight-hectare site has 161 pitches with 34 for touring, on level grass with 6/10A electricity. The site is only 75 minutes from Calais, 18 km. from the motorway. An excellent covered pool complex has been added, including a flume, jacuzzi and pool for toddlers, and a fitness room and sauna. This area is particularly good for cycling with several level, traffic-free routes nearby. The Bay of the Somme, St Valéry, watersports and the cathedral city of Amiens are all close.

You might like to know

The campsite is just 900 m. from the Marquenterre Ornithological Park, an important migratory stopover where over 350 different species of bird have been seen. A nearby cycle route leads to beautiful sandy beaches.

- ⊘ Environmental accreditation
- ⊘ Reduced energy/water consumption policy
- ⊘ Recycling and reusing policy
- ⊘ Information about walking and cycling
- ⊘ Footpaths within 500 m. of the site
- ⊘ Fishing within 1 km.
- ⊘ Riding or pony trekking within 1 km.
- ○ Direct river or lake access
- ⊘ Area of outstanding natural beauty or National Park within 10 km.
- ⊘ Wildlife haven (on site or within 1 km)
- ○ Public transport
- ⊘ Dogs welcome

Camp du Domaine

B.P. 207 La Favière, 2581 Route de Bénat, F-83230 Bormes-les-Mimosas (Var)
t: 04 94 71 03 12   e: mail@campdudomaine.com
alanrogers.com/FR83120   www.campdudomaine.com

Accommodation: ☑ Pitch ☑ Mobile home/chalet ○ Hotel/B&B ○ Apartment

Camp du Domaine, 3 km. south of Le Lavandou, is a large, attractive beachside site with 1,320 pitches set in 45 hectares of pinewood, yet surprisingly it does not give the impression of being so big. The pitches are large and most are reasonably level; 800 have 10A electricity. The most popular pitches are beside the beach, but those furthest away are generally larger and have more shade. Amongst the trees, many pitches are more suitable for tents. The price for each pitch is the same – whether smaller but near the beach, or larger under shade. The beach is the attraction and everyone tries to get close. American motorhomes are not accepted. Despite its size, the site does not feel too busy, except perhaps around the supermarket. Its popularity makes early reservation necessary over a long season (about mid June to mid September) since regular clients book from season to season. A good range of languages are spoken. A member of Leading Campings group.

You might like to know

Situated in a vast, wooded park with direct beach access, Camp du Domaine is ideal for appreciating the stunning Mediterranean vegetation, most notably at Bormes les Mimosas and the Domaine du Rayol botanic garden.

○ Environmental accreditation
☑ Reduced energy/water consumption policy
☑ Recycling and reusing policy
☑ Information about walking and cycling
☑ Footpaths within 500 m. of the site
☑ Fishing within 1 km.
○ Riding or pony trekking within 1 km.
○ Direct river or lake access
☑ Area of outstanding natural beauty or National Park within 10 km.
☑ Wildlife haven (on site or within 1 km)
☑ Public transport
☑ Dogs welcome

Facilities: Ten modern, well used but clean toilet blocks. Mostly Turkish WCs. Facilities for disabled visitors (but steep steps). Baby room. Washing machines. Fridge hire. Well stocked supermarket, bars, pizzeria. No swimming pool. Several excellent play areas for all ages. Activities and entertainment for children and teenagers (July/Aug). Tennis. Boats, pedaloes for hire. Wide range of watersports. New water games and fitness area. Multisports courts (one indoor for wet or hot weather) for football, basketball. Only gas and electric barbecues are allowed. Direct beach access. Dogs are not accepted 13/7-17/8. Free WiFi at the Tennis Bar (rest of site charged). Off site: Bicycle hire 2.5 km. Riding and golf 15 km.

Open: 28 March - 31 October.

Directions: From Bormes-les-Mimosas, head east on D559 to Le Lavandou. At roundabout, turn off D559 towards the sea on road signed Favière. After 2 km. turn left at site signs.
GPS: 43.11779, 6.35176

Charges guide

Per unit incl. 2 persons and electricity	€ 31,00 - € 49,00
extra person	€ 6,50 - € 11,50
child (2-7 yrs)	no charge - € 5,60
dog (not 13/7-17/8)	no charge

Facilities: Two sanitary blocks with washbasins and showers in cubicles and facilities for children and disabled visitors. Laundry. Bar, snack bar (July/Aug and weekends). Covered, heated swimming pool and children's pool (1/4-30/9). Play area. Games room. Trampoline. Volleyball. Pétanque pitch. Activity and entertainment programme (July/Aug). WiFi (charged). Mobile homes and chalets for rent. Fishing. Small animal farm. Off site: Restaurant 500 m. Shops 1 km. Apremont 12 km. Bicycle hire 15 km. Beaches and riding 20 km. Golf 30 km. Noirmoutier 40 km. Puy du Fou 70 km. Cycling and walking tracks.

Open: All year.

Directions: From Challans, head south on D2948 towards Aizenay. On reaching St Christophe du Ligneron, follow signs to site.

GPS: 46.81511, -1.77472

Charges guide

Per unit incl. 2 persons and electricity € 14,00 - € 21,00
extra person € 3,10 - € 4,50
child (under 7 yrs) € 2,80 - € 3,50
dog € 3,00

France – Saint Christophe-du-Ligneron

Camping du Domaine de Bellevue

Bellevue de Ligneron, F-85670 Saint Christophe-du-Ligneron (Vendée)
t: 02 51 93 30 66 e: campingdebellevue85@orange.fr
alanrogers.com/FR85385 www.vendee-camping-bellevue.com

Accommodation: ☑ Pitch ☑ Mobile home/chalet ○ Hotel/B&B ○ Apartment

Domaine de Bellevue is a family site located in the northern Vendée, close to the town of Challans (famous for its market), and around 20 minutes from the broad, sandy beaches at Saint-Gilles-Croix-de-Vie. There are 126 large (minimum 110 sq.m) pitches here, 30 for tourers, all fully serviced with 16A electricity, dispersed around a large park, which has two generous fishing ponds stocked with carp and other species. An entertainment programme runs during July and August and includes special activities for children. There is a range of mobile homes, chalets and bungalow-style tents for rent. The nearest shops are around 1 km. away and there is a restaurant some 500 m. distant. The Vendée is renowned for its excellent cycle trails and several of these run close to the site. Other places of interest include the fine 16th-century château at Apremont and the island of Noirmoutier to the north. The Puy du Fou theme park and evening spectacular is some 70 km. away.

You might like to know

A tranquil site surrounded by nature, with two fishing ponds and an animal park (chickens, goats, a pony and a pig).

○ Environmental accreditation
☑ Reduced energy/water consumption policy
☑ Recycling and reusing policy
☑ Information about walking and cycling
☑ Footpaths within 500 m. of the site
☑ Fishing within 1 km.
○ Riding or pony trekking within 1 km.
☑ Direct river or lake access
○ Area of outstanding natural beauty or National Park within 10 km.
☑ Wildlife haven (on site or within 1 km)
○ Public transport
☑ Dogs welcome

Facilities:
The fully equipped, airy toilet block includes all washbasins in cabins, provision for disabled visitors (key from reception), baby room and laundry. Bar (20/4-28/9) and restaurant (15/5-10/9) with terrace overlooking the lake. Takeaway (15/5-10/9). Two small play areas. Games and TV room. Canoeing and lake swimming. Programme of activities for children and adults in high season. WiFi (charged). Off site: Weekly markets in nearby Bruyères, Corcieux and St Dié. Riding 12 km. Golf 30 km.

Open: 18 April - 28 September.

Directions: From Épinal, exit N57 on N420 for St Dié and follow signs until you pick up signs for Bruyères. Lac du Messires is signed as you leave Bruyères on D423, at Laveline go south to Herpelmont and site.

GPS: 48.1787, 6.74309

Charges guide

Per unit incl. 2 persons and electricity	€ 19,00 - € 26,50
extra person	€ 4,00 - € 5,70
child (6-12 yrs)	€ 3,00 - € 5,00
dog	€ 3,00 - € 4,00

France – Herpelmont

Camping Domaine des Messires

1 rue des Messires, F-88600 Herpelmont (Vosges)
t: 03 29 58 56 29 e: mail@domainedesmessires.com
alanrogers.com/FR88070 www.domainedesmessires.com

Accommodation: ✓ Pitch ✓ Mobile home/chalet ○ Hotel/B&B ○ Apartment

Nestling in woods beside a lake, des Messires is a haven of peace and tranquillity and is perfect for nature lovers – not only are there birds and flowers but beavers, too. The Vosges is famous for its mountains and you can easily explore the Moselle vineyards and the medieval villages with their old walls and storks on chimneys. The 114 good sized and serviced pitches are on grass over stone, with some directly by the lakeside, excellent for fishing. When the day is over, enjoy a leisurely meal at the welcoming restaurant overlooking the lake or relax in the bar. There are 22 mobile homes for rent. Torches may be needed. For the more active, canoes are available free of charge in low season; swim in the lake or visit the nearby partner site for a swim in their pool. It is possible to walk or cycle around the lake. Should the weather be inclement, try some of the old-fashioned wooden games, play indoor minigolf or watch the satellite TV in the lounge with its open fire, near the bar.

You might like to know

This is a beautiful wooded site, where you will be welcomed not only by the birds, but by the beavers too.

- ○ Environmental accreditation
- ○ Reduced energy/water consumption policy
- ○ Recycling and reusing policy
- ✓ Information about walking and cycling
- ✓ Footpaths within 500 m. of the site
- ✓ Fishing within 1 km.
- ✓ Riding or pony trekking within 1 km.
- ✓ Direct river or lake access
- ✓ Area of outstanding natural beauty or National Park within 10 km.
- ✓ Wildlife haven (on site or within 1 km)
- ○ Public transport
- ✓ Dogs welcome

Ireland – Cahir

The Apple Camping & Caravan Park

Moorstown, Cahir (Co. Tipperary)
t: 052 744 1459   e: con@theapplefarm.com
alanrogers.com/IR9410   www.theapplefarm.com

Accommodation: ☑ Pitch ○ Mobile home/chalet ○ Hotel/B&B ○ Apartment

This fruit farm and campsite combination offers an idyllic country holiday venue in one of the most delightful situations imaginable. For touring units only, it is located off the N24, midway between Clonmel and Cahir. The park has 32 pitches in a secluded situation behind the barns, set among trees and shrubs. They are mostly grass with 14 hardstandings and 28 electricity connections (13A Europlug). Entrance is by way of a 300 m. drive flanked by the orchard fields and various non-fruit tree species, which are named and of interest to guests who are free to spend time walking the paths around the farm. Award-winning apple juice, cordials, jams, etc. are also sold by Con and Noreen in the farm shop. Reception is housed with the other site facilities in a large barn. Although a rather unusual arrangement, it is central and effective. The towns of Cahir and Clonmel are of historic interest and the countryside around boasts rivers, mountains, Celtic culture and scenic drives.

Facilities: Heated toilet facilities, kept very clean, comprise showers, washbasins with mirrors, electric points, etc. in functional units occupying two corners of the large floor space. Facilities for disabled visitors. Also in the barn are dishwashing sinks, washing machine and a fridge/freezer for campers to use. Good drive-on motorcaravan service point. Good tennis court (free). Play area. Dogs are not accepted. WiFi (free). Off site: Fishing, golf, and riding 6 km. Bicycle hire 9 km.

Open: 1 May - 30 September.

Directions: Park is 300 m. off main N24, 9.6 km. west of Clonmel, 6.4 km. east of Cahir. From M8 motorway take exit 10 and follow signs for Clonmel.
GPS: 52.37663, -7.84262

Charges guide

Per unit incl. 2 persons and electricity	€ 6,50
extra person	€ 7,00
child	€ 4,50

You might like to know

Surrounded by abundant orchards, you can sit back and relax and try some of the produce from the farm shop, including, of course, apple juice and cider!

○ Environmental accreditation
☑ Reduced energy/water consumption policy
☑ Recycling and reusing policy
☑ Information about walking and cycling
○ Footpaths within 500 m. of the site
○ Fishing within 1 km.
○ Riding or pony trekking within 1 km.
○ Direct river or lake access
○ Area of outstanding natural beauty or National Park within 10 km.
☑ Wildlife haven (on site or within 1 km)
○ Public transport
○ Dogs welcome

Ireland – Caherdaniel

Wave Crest Caravan & Camping Park

Caherdaniel (Co. Kerry)
t: 066 947 5188 e: wavecrest@eircom.net
alanrogers.com/IR9560 www.wavecrestcamping.com

Accommodation: ◉ Pitch ○ Mobile home/chalet ○ Hotel/B&B ○ Apartment

It would be difficult to imagine a more dramatic location than Wave Crest's on the Ring of Kerry coast. Huge boulders and rocky outcrops tumble from the park entrance on the N70 down to the seashore which forms the most southern promontory on the Ring of Kerry. There are spectacular views from the park across Kenmare Bay to the Beara peninsula. Sheltering on grass patches in small coves that nestle between the rocks and shrubbery, are 40 hardstanding pitches and 23 on grass offering seclusion. Electricity connections are available (13A). This park would suit older people looking for a quiet, relaxed atmosphere. A unique feature is the TV room, an old stone farm building with a thatched roof. Its comfortable interior includes a stone fireplace heated by a converted cast iron marker buoy. Caherdaniel is known for its cheerful little pubs and distinguished restaurant. The Derrynane National Park Nature Reserve is only a few kilometres away, as is Derrynane Cove and Bay.

You might like to know

Boat launching and mooring are available for visitors who want to enjoy the Irish coast from the sea.

- ◉ Environmental accreditation
- ◉ Reduced energy/water consumption policy
- ◉ Recycling and reusing policy
- ◉ Information about walking and cycling
- ○ Footpaths within 500 m. of the site
- ○ Fishing within 1 km.
- ◉ Riding or pony trekking within 1 km.
- ○ Direct river or lake access
- ◉ Area of outstanding natural beauty or National Park within 10 km.
- ◉ Wildlife haven (on site or within 1 km)
- ○ Public transport
- ◉ Dogs welcome

Facilities: Two blocks house the sanitary and laundry facilities and include hot showers on payment (€ 1). Small shop, restaurant and takeaway service (June-Sept). Small play area. Fishing and boat launching. WiFi throughout (charged). Boat trips from the site. Off site: Riding 1 km. Bicycle hire and golf 10 km. Small beach near and Derrynane Hotel with bar and restaurant.

Open: All year.

Directions: On the N70 (Ring of Kerry), 1.5 km. east of Caherdaniel.

GPS: 51.75881, -10.09112

Charges guide

Per unit incl. 2 persons and electricity	€ 28,00
extra person	€ 6,00
child	€ 2,00

Facilities: Toilet and shower facilities were clean when we visited. Modern and well equipped campers' kitchen and dining area. Comfortable campers' sitting room. Laundry facilities with washing machines and dryer. Motorcaravan services. Picnic and barbecue facilities. Fishing and boat launching from site. Playing field. WiFi throughout. Off site: Bicycle hire 800 m. Riding 3 km. Golf 14 km. Pubs, restaurants and shops 15 minutes walk. Watersports, birdwatching, walking and photography. Local cruises to Skelligs Rock with free transport to and from the port for walkers and cyclists.

Open: 15 March - 15 October.

Directions: Park is 300 m. off the N70 Ring of Kerry road, 800 m. southwest of Cahirciveen (or Cahersiveen) on the road towards Waterville.
GPS: 51.941517, -10.24465

Charges guide

Per unit incl. 2 persons
and electricity € 27,00

extra person € 6,00

No credit cards.

Ireland – *Cahirciveen*

Mannix Point Camping & Caravan Park

Cahirciveen (Co. Kerry)
t: 066 947 2806   e: mortimer@campinginkerry.com
alanrogers.com/IR9610   www.campinginkerry.com

Accommodation: ☑ Pitch ○ Mobile home/chalet ○ Hotel/B&B ○ Apartment

A tranquil, beautifully located seashore park, it is no exaggeration to describe Mannix Point as a nature lovers' paradise. Situated in one of the most spectacular parts of the Ring of Kerry, overlooking the bay and Valentia Island, the rustic seven-acre park commands splendid views. The park road meanders through the level site and offers 42 pitches of various sizes and shapes, many with shelter and seclusion and all with 10A electricity. A charming, converted fisherman's cottage provides facilities including reception, excellent campers' kitchen and a cosy sitting room with turf fire. The knowledgeable and hospitable owner is a Bord Fáilte registered local tour guide. A keen gardener, Mortimer Moriarty laid out the site over 20 years ago and his intention to cause as little disruption to nature as possible has succeeded. The site opens directly onto marshland which teems with wildlife (a two-acre nature reserve). A viewing platform allows observation of seals and birdlife.

You might like to know

Valentia is an island of great character and beauty, accessible in summer by ferry and throughout the year by a road bridge. The sub-tropical gardens of Glanleam House are a 'must see'.

○ Environmental accreditation
○ Reduced energy/water consumption policy
☑ Recycling and reusing policy
☑ Information about walking and cycling
☑ Footpaths within 500 m. of the site
☑ Fishing within 1 km.
☑ Riding or pony trekking within 1 km.
○ Direct river or lake access
☑ Area of outstanding natural beauty or National Park within 10 km.
☑ Wildlife haven (on site or within 1 km)
○ Public transport
☑ Dogs welcome

Facilities:

Nine modern toilet blocks are maintained to a very high standard with hot showers and a high proportion of British style toilets. Pleasant facilities for disabled visitors. Laundry. Range of shops. Several bars, restaurants and takeaways. Five beach bars/snack bars. Enormous swimming pool complex with slides and flumes. Several play areas. Tennis. Surfboard and catamaran hire. Wide range of organised entertainment. WiFi (charged). Special area and facilities for dog owners (also beach area). Off site: Fishing 1 km. Riding 7 km. Golf 10 km.

Open: 12 April - 30 September.

Directions: From A4 motorway, take Jesolo exit. After Jesolo continue towards Punta Sabbioni. Site is clearly signed to the left towards the end of this road, close to the Venice ferries.

GPS: 45.43750, 12.43805

Charges guide

Per unit incl. 2 persons
and electricity € 21,10 - € 48,50

extra person € 4,70 - € 10,90

child or senior
(2-5 and over 60) € 3,90 - € 8,70

dog € 1,50 - € 5,10

Italy – Punta Sabbioni

Camping Marina di Venezia

Via Montello 6, I-30013 Punta Sabbioni (Veneto)
t: 041 530 2511   e: camping@marinadivenezia.it
alanrogers.com/IT60450   www.marinadivenezia.it

Accommodation: ☑ Pitch ☑ Mobile home/chalet ○ Hotel/B&B ○ Apartment

This is an amazingly large site (2,915 pitches) with every conceivable facility. It has a pleasant feel, with cheerful staff and no notion of being overcrowded, even when full. Marina di Venezia has the advantage of being within walking distance of the ferry to Venice. It will appeal in particular to those who enjoy an extensive range of entertainment and activities and a lively atmosphere. Individual pitches are spacious and out on sandy or grassy ground; most are separated by trees or hedges. All are equipped with 10A electricity and water. The site's excellent sandy beach is one of the widest along this stretch of coast and has five pleasant beach bars. The 15,000 sq.m. wide, multi-level AquaMarina Park has exceptional facilities – a feature pool for children with slides and a huge cascade complex, an Olympic size pool with massage jets, a lagoon with disability access, and a wave pool with a beach. This is a very efficiently run site with committed management and staff.

You might like to know

The campsite is located on a beautiful, sandy beach with natural dunes and clean, warm water (Blue Flag). There are many cycling routes for exploring the lagoon with its unique flora and fauna. A luxurious pine wood surrounds the campsite.

- ☑ Environmental accreditation
- ☑ Reduced energy/water consumption policy
- ☑ Recycling and reusing policy
- ☑ Information about walking and cycling
- ○ Footpaths within 500 m. of the site
- ☑ Fishing within 1 km.
- ○ Riding or pony trekking within 1 km.
- ○ Direct river or lake access
- ☑ Area of outstanding natural beauty or National Park within 10 km.
- ☑ Wildlife haven (on site or within 1 km)
- ☑ Public transport
- ☑ Dogs welcome

Facilities: Modern toilet block with all necessary facilities including those for babies and disabled visitors. Motorcaravan services. Small shop (15/3-5/11). Restaurant and bar (30/3-31/10). Small heated outdoor swimming pool (1/4-30/9). Play area. WiFi throughout (free). Charcoal barbecues not permitted. Off site: Bus stop 200 m. Large swimming pool 200 m. (May onwards; free to campers). Historical town of Meran 7 km. Museums. Golf and bicycle hire 2 km. Fishing 3 km. Hiking, Tennis. Paragliding. Rock climbing. Canoeing. Nature parks. Cable car.

Open: 1 March - 15 November.

Directions: Leave A22 Brenner motorway at Bozen Süd. Take expressway towards Meran. At the Lana-Burgstall exit turn left. After 250 m. take first right and follow signs to site.

GPS: 46.611151, 11.174434

Charges guide

Per unit incl. 2 persons and electricity € 33,00 - € 37,00	
extra person € 7,00	
child (5-10 yrs) € 4,00	

Italy – Lana

Camping Arquin

Feldgatterweg 25, I-39011 Lana (Trentino - Alto Adige)
t: 0473 561 187 e: info@camping-arquin.it
alanrogers.com/IT61865 www.camping-arquin.it

Accommodation: ☑ Pitch ○ Mobile home/chalet ○ Hotel/B&B ○ Apartment

Camping Arquin is in the South Tirol (Alto Adige) where the majority of the population speak German. It is open from early March to mid November and lies in an open valley surrounded by orchards, beyond which are high mountains. This is a region of natural beauty and is famous for its flowery meadows. The site is close to the village of Lana, one of the largest in the South Tirol and famous for its Mediterranean climate. There are 120 sunny, level, grass pitches up to 100 sq.m, all with 6A electricity and many are fully serviced. There is a wide range of marked footpaths and cycling routes. This is a good base for active families wishing to explore the local area on foot, by bicycle, in the car, by bus or by train (Bolzano 20 km). The higher reaches of the mountains can be accessed by cable car. This area is also known for its thermal springs and baths. The interesting old town of Meran is only 7 km. away and is accessible by bus.

You might like to know

Highly recommended visits include the Ultental with traditional farms or the Passeiertal with mountain passes (Jaufenpass-Timmelsjoch) – a popular spot for mountain bikers.

- ☑ Environmental accreditation
- ○ Reduced energy/water consumption policy
- ☑ Recycling and reusing policy
- ☑ Information about walking and cycling
- ☑ Footpaths within 500 m. of the site
- ○ Fishing within 1 km.
- ○ Riding or pony trekking within 1 km.
- ○ Direct river or lake access
- ☑ Area of outstanding natural beauty or National Park within 10 km.
- ○ Wildlife haven (on site or within 1 km)
- ☑ Public transport
- ☑ Dogs welcome

Facilities: One luxury underground block is in the centre of the site. 16 private units are available. Excellent facilities for disabled visitors. Fairy tale facilities for children. Infrared sensors, underfloor heating and gently curved floors to prevent slippery surfaces. Constant fresh air ventilation. Washing machines and large drying room. Sauna. Supermarket. Quality restaurant and bar with terrace. Entertainment programme. Miniclub. Children's adventure park and play room. Special rooms for ski equipment. Torches useful. WiFi (charged). Apartments and mobile homes for rent. Off site: Riding alongside site. 18-hole golf course (discounts) and fishing 1 km. Bicycle hire and lake swimming 2 km. ATM 3 km. Walks. Skiing in winter. Buses to cable cars and ski lifts.

Open: All year
excl. 2 November - 20 December.

Directions: From A22-E45 take Bolzano Nord exit. Take road for Prato Isarco/Blumau, then road for Fie/Völs. Road divides suddenly – if you miss the left fork as you enter a tunnel (Altopiano dello Sciliar/Schlerngebiet) you will pay a heavy price in extra kilometres. Enjoy the climb to Völs am Schlern and site is well signed.

GPS: 46.53344, 11.53335

Charges guide

Per unit incl. 2 persons € 21,10 - € 37,90	
extra person € 7,00 - € 10,20	
child (2-16 yrs) € 3,60 - € 8,10	
electricity (per kWh) € 0,60	
dog € 3,50 - € 5,20	

Camping Seiser Alm

Saint Konstantin 16, I-39050 Völs am Schlern (Trentino - Alto Adige)
t: 047 170 6459   e: info@camping-seiseralm.com
alanrogers.com/IT62040   www.camping-seiseralm.com

Accommodation: ☑ Pitch ☑ Mobile home/chalet ○ Hotel/B&B ☑ Apartment

What an amazing experience awaits you at Seiser Alm! Elisabeth and Erhard Mahlknecht have created a superb site in the magnificent Südtirol region of the Dolomite mountains. Towering peaks provide a wonderful backdrop when you dine in the charming, traditional-style restaurant on the upper terrace. Here you will also find the bar, shop and reception. The 150 touring pitches are of a very high standard with 16A electricity supply, 120 with gas, water, drainage and satellite connections. Guests were delighted with the site when we visited, many coming to walk or cycle, some just to enjoy the surroundings. There are countless things to see and do here. Enjoy the grand 18-hole golf course alongside the site or join the organised excursions and activities. Local buses and cable cars provide an excellent service for summer visitors and skiers alike (discounts are available). If you wish for quiet, quality camping in a crystal clean environment, then visit this immaculate site.

You might like to know

The Seiser Alm campsite is located in the beautiful landscape surrounding Alpe di Siusi, with a fine view of the towering Sciliar Massif, the symbol of Alto Adige.

○ Environmental accreditation
☑ Reduced energy/water consumption policy
☑ Recycling and reusing policy
○ Information about walking and cycling
☑ Footpaths within 500 m. of the site
☑ Fishing within 1 km.
☑ Riding or pony trekking within 1 km.
○ Direct river or lake access
☑ Area of outstanding natural beauty or National Park within 10 km.
☑ Wildlife haven (on site or within 1 km)
☑ Public transport
☑ Dogs welcome

Italy – Fucine di Ossana

Camping Cevedale

Via di Sotto Pila 4, I-38026 Fucine di Ossana (Trentino - Alto Adige)
t: 046 375 1630 e: info@campingcevedale.it
alanrogers.com/IT62110 www.campingcevedale.it

Accommodation: ⦿ Pitch ⦿ Mobile home/chalet ○ Hotel/B&B ○ Apartment

Facilities: Two sanitary blocks with mainly Turkish style toilets are well maintained, modern and spotlessly clean. They include hot water for showers and basins, heating in winter, washing machine and dryer. Small shop. Pleasant bar which serves snacks. Play area with tables and barbecues. Internet access. WiFi throughout (free). Adventure sport courses arranged. Bicycle hire. Dogs are not accepted. Off site: Shops, restaurants and bars in the two nearby villages 1 km. Golf 500 m. Riding 3 km. Skiing 10 km. Trekking, cycling, climbing, rope courses, abseiling, canyoning, rafting, fishing nearby.

Open: All year.

Directions: From the A22 (Brenner-Modena) take exit for San Michele, north of Trento, then SS43 north for 43 km. to Cles. Turn east on SS42 for 26 km. to Fucine. Continue through village and turn south on SP202 (Ossana). Follow signs for campsite (ignore sat nav!). The entrance is next to the bridge just below the castle.

GPS: 46.30834, 10.73361

Charges guide

Per unit incl. 2 persons and electricity	€ 25,00 - € 32,00
extra person	€ 8,00 - € 9,00
child (3-8 yrs)	€ 6,00 - € 7,00

Nestled under a castle and close to a tiny village, Camping Cevedale has a European atmosphere with very little English spoken, except by Maura, who runs the site. The 197 pitches are grouped in two areas on either side of a fast flowing river (fenced) which can be noisy. The touring pitches, all with electricity (only 2A), are shaded, on grass and slope somewhat; they are in various areas among the well kept seasonal caravans. Some campers come here every holiday and most have built little wooden chalets next to their caravans. This area is known for skiing in winter, rafting, adventure sports, mountain bike riding and trekking. Adventure sport courses are arranged by the management, and access to this kind of activity is one of the site's strengths.

You might like to know

We are one of the few Italian campsites which have the European ECOLABEL trademark.

- ⦿ Environmental accreditation
- ⦿ Reduced energy/water consumption policy
- ⦿ Recycling and reusing policy
- ⦿ Information about walking and cycling
- ⦿ Footpaths within 500 m. of the site
- ⦿ Fishing within 1 km.
- ⦿ Riding or pony trekking within 1 km.
- ⦿ Direct river or lake access
- ⦿ Area of outstanding natural beauty or National Park within 10 km.
- ○ Wildlife haven (on site or within 1 km)
- ⦿ Public transport
- ○ Dogs welcome

Facilities: Four modern sanitary blocks spaced through the site have mostly British style WCs, cold water in washbasins and hot, pre-mixed water in showers and sinks. Facilities for disabled visitors. Washing machine. Motorcaravan services. Bar. Happy Pig restaurant and takeaway. Shop (basics, 1/6-20/9). Two swimming pools (20/5-30/9). Play area. Tennis. Boules. Entertainment in high season. Excursions. WiFi over part of site (charged). Bungalows and chalets to rent. Off site: Monti Sibillini National Park is nearby (excursions organised). Walking and cycling opportunities. Fishing and bicycle hire 10 km. Kayaking 20 km. Hang-gliding 25 km.

Open: 1 April - 30 September.

Directions: Approach on the A14-E55 down the east coast, then via autoroute approach on SS17 from Civitanova Marche to Polverina, then left on the SS209. Look for Campeggio sign (no site name) 8 km. from Preci. Ensure you leave the site down the hill on the unsigned one way system.

GPS: 42.888, 13.01464

Charges guide

Per unit incl. 2 persons and electricity	€ 20,50 - € 35,00
extra person	€ 6,00 - € 9,50
child (3-12 yrs)	€ 3,00 - € 6,00

Italy – Castelvecchio di Preci

Camping Il Collaccio

Localitá Collaccio, I-06047 Castelvecchio di Preci (Umbria)
t: 074 393 9005   e: info@ilcollaccio.com
alanrogers.com/IT66560   www.ilcollaccio.com

Accommodation: ☑ Pitch ☑ Mobile home/chalet ○ Hotel/B&B ○ Apartment

Castelvecchio di Preci is tucked away in the tranquil heights of the mountainous Umbrian countryside, as is Camping Il Collaccio, which is set on a hillside. The 104 terraced touring pitches, with shade and 6A electricity, have stunning views. The friendly Baldoni family have run the business well for over 30 years. A dip in the pools is wonderfully cooling in summer and an evening meal whilst taking in the views of the lush green vegetation of the surrounding hills is a must. Very popular salami making and Umbrian cookery courses take place over Easter and New Year, and the products can be bought in the shop and sampled in the excellent restaurant. It is too high for vines here, but try the Umbrian wines carried in the cellar. Another interesting feature is truffle cultivation on the lower slopes of the site. Thousands of trees have been planted here over the years. A clean, crisp and tranquil place, with a really pleasant feel – we liked it here!

You might like to know

Relax and enjoy the beautiful views, from the swimming pool or from the restaurant terrace.

○ Environmental accreditation
☑ Reduced energy/water consumption policy
☑ Recycling and reusing policy
☑ Information about walking and cycling
○ Footpaths within 500 m. of the site
○ Fishing within 1 km.
○ Riding or pony trekking within 1 km.
○ Direct river or lake access
☑ Area of outstanding natural beauty or National Park within 10 km.
☑ Wildlife haven (on site or within 1 km)
○ Public transport
☑ Dogs welcome

Facilities: Laundry. Shop. Café/bar. Restaurant and pizzeria. Rental accommodation. Bicycle hire. WiFi. Off site: Riding 100 m. Boat trips and hire. Fishing. Steam train. Archaeological sites.

Open: 1 April - 15 October.

Directions: Camping La Pineta is 80 km. north east of Cagliari. From Cagliari take SS125 towards Olbia. Just after Tertenia follow signs to Barisardo. On entering Barisardo follow signs on right to site in 3 km.

GPS: 39.82028, 9.67032

Charges guide

Per unit incl. 2 persons and electricity € 15,00 - € 33,50	
extra person € 4,00 - € 9,00	
child (3-10 yrs) € 2,50 - € 6,00	
dog no charge	

Italy – Bari Sardo

Camping La Pineta

Localitá Planargia, I-08042 Bari Sardo (Sardinia)
t: 078 229 372 e: info@campingbungalowlapineta.it
alanrogers.com/IT69715 www.campingbungalowlapineta.it

Accommodation: ☑ Pitch ☑ Mobile home/chalet ○ Hotel/B&B ○ Apartment

Camping La Pineta is a small, family run campsite on the island of Sardinia. It lies just 400 metres from the clean, safe, Mediterranean beach of Planargia. Set amongst mature pine and eucalyptus trees this 1.5-hectare campsite has a mixture of mobile homes and shaded touring pitches, some of which are suitable for tents, others can accommodate caravans or motorcaravans. All have electricity points and water close by. The restaurant, café/bar, pizzeria and mini-market cater for most needs, whilst the small town of Barisardo (3.5 kilometres) has a wider range of amenities. The staff will assist with ferry and flight bookings if required. La Pineta is in a quiet, rural location but would make a good base for exploring the varied coastline and Saracen towers. A short distance inland, you are in the mountainous areas with a multitude of geologically interesting natural formations. Many places can be reached by foot, by mountain bike or even on horseback.

You might like to know

Why not discover the wild, unspoilt territory of the Ogliastra on the charming Trenino Verde, one of Italy's oldest railways.

- ☑ Environmental accreditation
- ☑ Reduced energy/water consumption policy
- ○ Recycling and reusing policy
- ☑ Information about walking and cycling
- ☑ Footpaths within 500 m. of the site
- ☑ Fishing within 1 km.
- ☑ Riding or pony trekking within 1 km.
- ○ Direct river or lake access
- ☑ Area of outstanding natural beauty or National Park within 10 km.
- ☑ Wildlife haven (on site or within 1 km)
- ☑ Public transport
- ☑ Dogs welcome

Facilities: Three sanitary blocks. One is newly renovated with private bathrooms, and facilities for children and disabled visitors. The two older blocks have mixed Turkish/British style toilets. Washing machine. Motorcaravan service point (extra charge). Shop, restaurant and snack bar/takeaway (10/5-30/9). Live music concerts. Dog beach. Miniclub and entertainment in high season. Tennis. Water aerobics. Sailing. Sub-aqua diving. Windsurfing school. Riding. Torches essential. Bicycle hire. WiFi over site (charged). Communal barbecue areas. Off site: Riding 500 m.

Open: 20 April - 12 October.

Directions: Site is in southeast corner of Sardinia in the north of the Costa Rei. From coast road SS125 or the SP97 at km. 6, take the turn to Villaggio Capo Ferrato. Site is well signed from here.
GPS: 39.2923, 9.5987

Charges guide

Per unit incl. 2 persons and electricity	€ 22,50 - € 50,50
extra person	€ 5,00 - € 14,00
child (1-9 yrs acc. to age)	€ 2,00 - € 10,00
dog	€ 3,00 - € 6,00

Italy – Muravera

Tiliguerta Camping Village

S.P. 97 km. 6 - Loc. Capo Ferrato, I-09043 Muravera (Sardinia)
t: 070 991 437   e: info@tiliguerta.com
alanrogers.com/IT69750   www.tiliguerta.com

Accommodation: ☑ Pitch ☑ Mobile home/chalet ☑ Hotel/B&B ○ Apartment

This family site situated at Capo Ferrato has changed its owners, name and direction (2011). The new owners have made many improvements, all of them in sympathy with the environment. The 186 reasonably sized pitches are on sand and have 3A electricity. Some have shade and views of the superb, fine beach and sea beyond. There are ten permanent pitches used by Italian units. The traditional site buildings are centrally located and contain a good quality restaurant. Shaded terraces allow comfortable viewing of the ambitious entertainment programme. Cars must be parked away from pitches. The staff are cheerful and English is spoken. Consideration is given to the environment at every turn. There are numerous activities on offer – basketball, beach volleyball, riding and watersports, and in high season yoga, tai-chi, Pilates and dancing are possible. We believe Tiliguerta is becoming a good quality, environmentally friendly site.

You might like to know

Tiliguerta is located in a protected wildlife area where a wealth of strikingly coloured marsh areas provide an ideal habitat for many species of birds, including flamingos, herons, egrets, black-winged stilts and cormorants.

○ Environmental accreditation
☑ Reduced energy/water consumption policy
☑ Recycling and reusing policy
☑ Information about walking and cycling
☑ Footpaths within 500 m. of the site
☑ Fishing within 1 km.
☑ Riding or pony trekking within 1 km.
○ Direct river or lake access
☑ Area of outstanding natural beauty or National Park within 10 km.
☑ Wildlife haven (on site or within 1 km)
☑ Public transport
☑ Dogs welcome

Facilities: The well maintained sanitary block in two parts includes a modern, heated unit with some washbasins in cubicles, and excellent, fully equipped cubicles for disabled visitors. The showers, facilities for babies, additional WCs and washbasins, plus laundry room are located below the central building which houses the shop, bar and restaurant. Motorcaravan services. Gas supplies. Indoor and outdoor play areas. Solar heated swimming pool (Easter-30/9). Paddling pool. WiFi (free). Off site: Bicycle hire. Golf, fishing and riding 8 km.

Open: 1 March - 8 November.

Directions: From Larochette take the CR118/N8 (towards Mersch) and just outside town turn right on CR119 towards Schrondweiler, site is 2 km. on right.

GPS: 49.79992, 6.19817

Charges guide

Per unit incl. 2 persons and electricity € 22,00 - € 32,00	
extra person € 10,00 - € 15,00	
child (4-17 yrs) € 5,00 - € 7,00	
dog € 1,50	

Luxembourg – Larochette

Camping Auf Kengert

Kengert, L-7633 Larochette-Medernach (Luxembourg)
t: 837186 e: info@kengert.lu
alanrogers.com/LU7640 www.kengert.lu

Accommodation: ☑ Pitch ☑ Mobile home/chalet ○ Hotel/B&B ○ Apartment

A friendly welcome awaits you at this peacefully situated, family run site, 2 km. from Larochette, which is 24 km. northeast of Luxembourg City, providing 180 individual pitches, all with electricity (16A Europlug). Some in a very shaded woodland setting, on a slight slope with fairly narrow access roads. There are also eight hardened pitches for motorcaravans on a flat area of grass, complete with motorcaravan service facilities. Further tent pitches are in an adjacent and more open meadow area. There are also site owned wooden chalets for rent. This site is popular in season, so early arrival is advisable, or you can reserve. The swimming pool is overlooked by a terrace with a well stocked shop, a restaurant and bar behind and a delightful children's indoor play area. In the meadow at the side of the site is a large sand-based adventure play park. Beyond that is a 'barefoot woodland walk' along which you can tread on a variety of natural surfaces - reflexology on the go!

You might like to know

A barefoot-walking track starts direct from the campsite, and nearby you can join the Mullerthal Trail hiking track to explore Luxembourg's Little Switzerland.

- ☑ Environmental accreditation
- ☑ Reduced energy/water consumption policy
- ☑ Recycling and reusing policy
- ☑ Information about walking and cycling
- ☑ Footpaths within 500 m. of the site
- ○ Fishing within 1 km.
- ○ Riding or pony trekking within 1 km.
- ○ Direct river or lake access
- ☑ Area of outstanding natural beauty or National Park within 10 km.
- ○ Wildlife haven (on site or within 1 km)
- ☑ Public transport
- ☑ Dogs welcome

Facilities:
Next to the reception is a heated sanitary block where some facilities are found, others including some showers are located under cover, outside. Showers are token operated, washbasins open style. Facilities may be stretched in high season. Laundry room. Gas supplies. Bar (all day in high season). Takeaway (high season except Sundays). Swimming and paddling in river. Three play areas (one with waterways, waterwheel and small pool). Bicycle hire. WiFi (1st hour free). Max. 1 dog. Off site: Fishing and golf 10 km.

Open: 29 March - 1 November.

Directions: From A26/E25 (Liège-Luxembourg) exit 54 travel to Bastogne. Then take N84/N15 towards Diekirch for 15 km. At crossroads turn left towards Wiltz following signs for Clervaux. Pass through Wiltz and into Weidingen, 500 m. after VW garage turn right on Wilderwiltz road. In Wilderwiltz follow signs for Enscherange where site is signed.

GPS: 50.00017, 5.99106

Charges guide

Per unit incl. 2 persons
and electricity € 16,00 - € 22,00

extra person € 5,00

child (0-15 yrs) € 2,20

dog (max. 1) € 5,00

No credit cards.

Camping Val d'Or

Um Gaertchen 2, L-9747 Enscherange (Luxembourg)
t: 920 691   e: valdor@pt.lu
alanrogers.com/LU7770 www.valdor.lu

Accommodation: ☑ Pitch   ☑ Mobile home/chalet   ○ Hotel/B&B   ☑ Apartment

Camping Val d'Or is one of those small, family run, countryside sites where you easily find yourself staying longer than planned. Set in four hectares of lush meadowland under a scattering of trees, the site is divided into two by the tree-lined Clerve river as it winds its way slowly through the site. A footbridge goes some way to joining the site together and there are two entrances for vehicles. There are 76 marked, level grass touring pitches, all with electricity (4-6A Europlug) and with some tree shade. Cars are parked away from the pitches. There are open views of the surrounding countryside with its wooded hills. The site's Dutch owners speak good English. Fred van Donk is active in the Luxembourg tourist industry. He is happy to give advice about this interesting, attractive and less well known region of Europe which is within easy reach of the Channel ports and the Netherlands. The site participates in the Wanderhütten scheme providing wooden huts for rent to hikers.

You might like to know

During the high season, there are guided walks to inform you about the development of the forest and help you make the most of this beautiful landscape.

☑ Environmental accreditation
☑ Reduced energy/water consumption policy
☑ Recycling and reusing policy
☑ Information about walking and cycling
☑ Footpaths within 500 m. of the site
○ Fishing within 1 km.
○ Riding or pony trekking within 1 km.
☑ Direct river or lake access
☑ Area of outstanding natural beauty or National Park within 10 km.
☑ Wildlife haven (on site or within 1 km)
☑ Public transport
☑ Dogs welcome

Facilities: Three clean, modern toilet blocks have family showers, hot water (on payment) and dishwashing sinks. One block has facilities for disabled visitors and a small laundry. Café/snack bar. Half size billiard tables. Play area. Football pitch. Tennis. Volleyball. Minigolf. Activities for children up to 12 yrs. (high season). Bicycle hire. WiFi over part of site (charged). Off site: Shops and restaurants in Bergen op Zoom. Riding 1 km. Golf 2 km. Sailing and boat launching 3 km. Fishing 5 km. Walking and cycle tracks.

Open: 1 May - 1 October.

Directions: Approaching from the south (Antwerp) use A4 motorway as far as the Bergen op Zoom exit and then follow signs to the Binnenschelde and campsite.

GPS: 51.469064, 4.322337

Charges guide

Per unit incl. 2 persons and electricity € 18,50	
extra person € 3,00	
child (3-10 yrs) € 2,00	
dog € 3,00	

Netherlands – Bergen op Zoom

Camping Uit en Thuis

Heimolen 56, NL-4625 DD Bergen op Zoom (Noord-Brabant)
t: 0164 233 391   e: info@campinguitenthuis.nl
alanrogers.com/NL5539   www.campinguitenthuis.nl

Accommodation: ☑ Pitch ☑ Mobile home/chalet ○ Hotel/B&B ○ Apartment

Camping Uit en Thuis (home and away) is a friendly, family run site close to the town of Bergen op Zoom. There is a choice of 80 sunny or shady touring pitches including eight with hardstanding. Most pitches have electricity (6A), water, drainage and cable TV connections. A number of fully equipped mobile homes are available for rent, as well as a simply furnished hikers' cabin (maximum three nights). There are also several pitches for cycle campers. On-site amenities include a popular snack bar/restaurant, which specialises in traditional Dutch cuisine. Bergen op Zoom is a pleasant Burgundian town, which was granted city status in 1266. It is a delightful place to explore with numerous historic buildings, many surrounding the Grote Markt, including the Markiezenhof Palace, which is now home to the city's cultural centre. The city borders the Binnenschelde Lake, popular for windsurfing and other watersports.

You might like to know

Camping Uit en Thuis sits in the undulating countryside of the Brabantse Wal, where guests can enjoy the wonderful views of this unique landscape.

- ○ Environmental accreditation
- ☑ Reduced energy/water consumption policy
- ☑ Recycling and reusing policy
- ☑ Information about walking and cycling
- ☑ Footpaths within 500 m. of the site
- ○ Fishing within 1 km.
- ☑ Riding or pony trekking within 1 km.
- ○ Direct river or lake access
- ☑ Area of outstanding natural beauty or National Park within 10 km.
- ☑ Wildlife haven (on site or within 1 km)
- ☑ Public transport
- ☑ Dogs welcome

Facilities: Two refurbished, heated sanitary blocks with some washbasins in cabins and controllable hot showers. Family shower rooms. Baby room. En-suite facilities for disabled visitors. Motorcaravan services. Shop for basics. Snack bar. TV in reception. Lake with fishing, boating, windsurfing. Football field. Riding. Nordic walking. Playground. Some entertainment for children (high season). Bicycle hire. Torch useful. WiFi over site (charged). Off site: Golf 10 km. Sub-tropical pool in Zuidlaren. Sprookjeshof theme park in Zuidlaren. City of Groningen.

Open: 1 April - 30 October.

Directions: From the A28 take exit 35 and continue towards Zuidlaren. Just before Zuidlaren follow signs for Schipborg and then site signs.

GPS: 53.079267, 6.665617

Charges guide

Per unit incl. 2 persons and electricity € 19,70 - € 23,65	
extra person (over 1 yr) € 3,35	
dog (max. 2) € 2,95	

No credit cards.

Netherlands – Schipborg

Camping De Vledders

Zeegserweg 2a, NL-9469 PL Schipborg (Drenthe)
t: 0504 091 489 e: info@devledders.nl
alanrogers.com/NL6130 www.devledders.nl

Accommodation: ☑ Pitch ☑ Mobile home/chalet ○ Hotel/B&B ○ Apartment

Camping De Vledders is set in the centre of one of the most beautiful nature reserves in Holland, between the Drentse Hondsrug and the Drentsche Aa river. This attractive site is landscaped with many varieties of trees and shrubs. There are 150 touring pitches (all with 6A electricity) on rectangular, grassy fields, separated by well kept hedges. The level pitches are around 100 sq.m. in size with some shade provided at the back from mature trees and hedges. Static units and seasonal pitches are on separate fields. In one corner of the site there is an attractive lake with sandy beaches. Boating, swimming and even windsurfing are possible on the lake. De Vledders is close to the sub-tropical pool at Zuidlaren and the Sprookjeshof, a theme park featuring all the well known fairy tales. Those looking for a quiet holiday in beautiful surroundings with many opportunities for walking and cycling will have a relaxing time here. The interesting old city of Groningen is only ten minutes drive away.

You might like to know

The surrounding countryside is idyllic – a succession of varied wildlife areas, an array of streams and small rivers and villages linked by cycle tracks and footpaths.

- ○ Environmental accreditation
- ☑ Reduced energy/water consumption policy
- ☑ Recycling and reusing policy
- ☑ Information about walking and cycling
- ☑ Footpaths within 500 m. of the site
- ☑ Fishing within 1 km.
- ☑ Riding or pony trekking within 1 km.
- ☑ Direct river or lake access
- ☑ Area of outstanding natural beauty or National Park within 10 km.
- ○ Wildlife haven (on site or within 1 km)
- ☑ Public transport
- ☑ Dogs welcome

Facilities

Facilities: Modern, heated sanitary facilities with provision for babies and disabled visitors. Washing machines and dryers. Clubhouse. Picnic tables. Recreation space. Volleyball. Sand quarry nature reserve. Bicycle hire. WiFi (charged). Off site: Swimming pool 800 m. (28/4-31/8). Walking and cycle routes nearby. Lunteren 2.5 km. Ede 6.8 km. Bardeveld 9.6 km.

Open: 1 March - 27 October.

Directions: De Rimboe is 25 km. northwest of Arnhem. From the E35 between Ede and Veenendaal turn north onto the A30. After 8 km. turn east to Lunteren. In Lunteren (Dorpstraat) follow signs for Boslaan. Site is opposite the bicycle shop.
GPS: 52.09221, 5.66294

Charges guide

Per unit incl. 2 persons and electricity	€ 15,30 - € 17,70
dog (max. 1)	€ 2,25

Netherlands – Lunteren

Camping De Rimboe

Boslaan 129, NL-6741 KG Lunteren (Gelderland)
t: 0318 482 371   e: info@campingderimboe.com
alanrogers.com/NL6331   www.campingderimboe.com

Accommodation: ☑ Pitch   ○ Mobile home/chalet   ○ Hotel/B&B   ○ Apartment

Camping De Rimboe is set in 10.5 hectares of sloping fields and mature woodland. The 140 touring pitches (90-150 sq.m) are either on grass, which has both sun and shade, or in the woods where there is an opportunity for free camping. All have a water point and 4/6A electricity. This is a peaceful site where visitors can relax, appreciate the natural environment and explore the area by foot or bicycle. As a contrast, the lively resort towns of Lunteren, Ede and Bardeveld are a short distance away. The site's recreational space provides opportunities for a variety of games and sports, and there is also a clubhouse and two play areas. There are many cycling and walking routes starting from the site or very close by. Bicycles can be rented and the walking paths are well signed. The modern, heated sanitary facilities have special provision for babies and visitors with disabilities. Behind the site there is a nature reserve which is a haven for flowers, plants and animals.

You might like to know

De Rimboe is beautifully situated in the forests near Lunteren. There is an open-air swimming pool nearby (800 m).

- ○ Environmental accreditation
- ☑ Reduced energy/water consumption policy
- ☑ Recycling and reusing policy
- ☑ Information about walking and cycling
- ☑ Footpaths within 500 m. of the site
- ○ Fishing within 1 km.
- ☑ Riding or pony trekking within 1 km.
- ○ Direct river or lake access
- ☑ Area of outstanding natural beauty or National Park within 10 km.
- ☑ Wildlife haven (on site or within 1 km)
- ○ Public transport
- ☑ Dogs welcome

Facilities: Good modern toilet block with hot, controllable showers, open style washbasins and well decorated facilities for children. Baby room and family shower rooms. Facilities for disabled visitors. Private sanitary facilities for rent. Laundry with washing machines and dryers. Shop for basics. Bar/restaurant. Heated outdoor swimming pool with paddling pool. Playing field. Indoor play hall. Bicycle hire. WiFi over site (charged). Entertainment team. Accommodation to rent. Dogs are not accepted. Off site: Riding 5 km. Fishing 7 km. Golf 15 km.

Open: 27 March - 26 October.

Directions: From the A1 take exit 28 and continue north on the N347 all the way to Lemele. Site is signed on the N347.

GPS: 52.46711, 6.42478

Charges guide

Per unit incl. 2 persons
and electricity € 19,85 - € 46,25

extra person € 4,40 - € 5,60

Netherlands – Lemele

Natuurcamping De Lemeler Esch

Lemelerweg 16, NL-8148 PC Lemele (Overijssel)
t: 0572 331 241 e: info@lemeleresch.nl
alanrogers.com/NL6460 www.lemeleresch.nl

Accommodation: ☑ Pitch ☑ Mobile home/chalet ○ Hotel/B&B ○ Apartment

This site is reminiscent of camping as it used to be, but with modern facilities including 190 spacious grass pitches for touring units, 114 with all comforts such as water, drainage, electricity, cable TV, WiFi and even a private bathroom if desired. The pitches are arranged on large grass meadows, some with shade from tall trees, others more in the open. The natural woodland setting gives this site a special atmosphere that allows children to explore and make friends. The good playground and a heated swimming pool are additional fun for children. This site will also appeal to adults as there are kilometres of cycling and walking tracks in the woods and across the moors. The 'back garden' of the site are the Lemelerberg and the Archemerberg and the beautiful Vecht river is also close. Lemeleresch offers plenty of opportunities for relaxed or active holidays on bike, on foot or on the waters of the Vecht.

You might like to know

The hiking network of Vechtdal Overijssel passes the site and leads to the famous Lemelerberg. The café is open all year round. Bungalows for rent all year.

☑ Environmental accreditation
☑ Reduced energy/water consumption policy
☑ Recycling and reusing policy
☑ Information about walking and cycling
☑ Footpaths within 500 m. of the site
☑ Fishing within 1 km.
☑ Riding or pony trekking within 1 km.
○ Direct river or lake access
☑ Area of outstanding natural beauty or National Park within 10 km.
☑ Wildlife haven (on site or within 1 km)
☑ Public transport
○ Dogs welcome

Facilities: Two large sanitary buildings (one new in 2012) with showers, toilets, washbasins in cabins, facilities for babies and for disabled visitors. Laundry room. Spacious reception area with supermarket, restaurant, bar and takeaway. Heated pool with children's pool and sliding roof. Lake swimming with sandy beach. New modern adventure play area and smaller play areas. Pétanque. Bicycle hire. Fishing pond. Tennis. Pets to stroke. Max. 1 dog. Luxury bungalows to rent (good views). New water spray park for children up to 13 yrs. Free WiFi over site. Off site: Riding 11 km. Golf 16 km.

Open: 29 March - 1 October.

Directions: From the A1 take exit 32 (Oldenzaal-Denekamp) and continue to Denekamp. Pass Denekamp and turn right at village of Noord-Deurningen and follow signs to site.
GPS: 52.39200, 7.04900

Charges guide

Per unit incl. 2 persons and 4A electricity	€ 27,00
incl. full services	€ 30,50
extra person	€ 4,25

Netherlands – Denekamp

Camping De Papillon

Kanaalweg 30, NL-7591 NH Denekamp (Overijssel)
t: 0541 351 670 e: info@depapillon.nl
alanrogers.com/NL6470 www.depapillon.nl

Accommodation: ☑ Pitch ☑ Mobile home/chalet ○ Hotel/B&B ○ Apartment

De Papillon is perhaps one of the best and most enjoyable campsites in the Netherlands. All 245 touring pitches are spacious (120-160 sq.m), all have electricity (4/10/16A), and 220 have water and drainage. An impressive, new sanitary block has state-of-the-art equipment and uses green technology. There is a new entertainment centre with outdoor auditorium for children, and the water play area by the adventure playground and covered, heated pool is most imaginative. The restored heathland area offers opportunities for nature lovers; there is also a large fishing lake and a swimming lake with beach area and activities. This friendly, welcoming site is well thought through with an eye for detail and an appreciation of nature and the environment. All buildings are heated by solar energy, and all waste is separated for recycling. This is a great destination for a holiday amongst nature and the countryside of the Twente region. A member of Leading Campings group.

You might like to know

The Almelo-Nordhorn canal runs past the site and is home to an abundance of flora and fauna – water lilies take over the canal and many birds nest along its banks. The German border is nearby, marked by an ancient lock.

- ○ Environmental accreditation
- ☑ Reduced energy/water consumption policy
- ☑ Recycling and reusing policy
- ☑ Information about walking and cycling
- ☑ Footpaths within 500 m. of the site
- ☑ Fishing within 1 km.
- ☑ Riding or pony trekking within 1 km.
- ☑ Direct river or lake access
- ○ Area of outstanding natural beauty or National Park within 10 km.
- ○ Wildlife haven (on site or within 1 km)
- ☑ Public transport
- ☑ Dogs welcome

Facilities: A single timber building complex at the entrance houses the reception office and the sanitary facilities, which provide for each sex, two WCs, and three open washbasins. Two unisex hot showers (on payment). Laundry. Small kitchen. Mini shop. Bread to order. Bicycle hire. WiFi (charged). Cabins for rent. Off site: Town facilities close. Local bus to glacier. Buar Glacier tours.

Open: All year.

Directions: Site is on the southern outskirts of Odda, signed off road to Buar, with a well marked access.

GPS: 60.05373, 6.54386

Charges guide

Per unit incl. 2 persons
and electricity NOK 200 - 210

Surcharge for credit cards.

Norway – Odda

Odda Camping

Jordalsveien 29, N-5750 Odda (Hordaland)
t: 41 32 16 10   e: post@oddacamping.no
alanrogers.com/NO2320   www.oddacamping.no

Accommodation: ☑ Pitch   ☑ Mobile home/chalet   ○ Hotel/B&B   ○ Apartment

The industrial town of Odda is bordered by the Folgefonna glacier and the Hardangervidda plateau. This site has been attractively developed on the town's southern outskirts. It occupies 2.5 acres of flat, mature woodland divided into small clearings by massive boulders. Access is by well tended tarmac roads that wind their way among the trees and boulders to 55 touring pitches including 36 with electricity. The site fills up in the evenings and can be crowded with facilities stretched from the end of June to early August. It also operates a motorcaravan facility on the quay in Odda for 40 units (coin-operated payment). The site is just over a kilometre from the town centre, on the shores of the Sandvin lake (good salmon and trout fishing) and on the minor road leading up the Buar Valley to the Buar glacier, Vidfoss Falls and Folgefonna ice cap. It is possible to walk to the ice face but in the later stages this is quite hard going!

You might like to know

Teenagers will love the challenge and excitement of paintball, where they can have hours of fun with friends.

○ Environmental accreditation
☑ Reduced energy/water consumption policy
☑ Recycling and reusing policy
☑ Information about walking and cycling
☑ Footpaths within 500 m. of the site
○ Fishing within 1 km.
○ Riding or pony trekking within 1 km.
○ Direct river or lake access
○ Area of outstanding natural beauty or National Park within 10 km.
☑ Wildlife haven (on site or within 1 km)
○ Public transport
○ Dogs welcome

Norway – Andenes

Andenes Camping

Storgata 53, N-8483 Andenes (Nordland)
t: 41 34 03 88   e: camping@whalesafari.no
alanrogers.com/NO2428   www.andenescamping.no

Accommodation: ☑ Pitch   ○ Mobile home/chalet   ○ Hotel/B&B   ○ Apartment

Lying on the exposed west coast of Andøy between the quiet main road and white sandy beaches, this site has an exceptional location for the midnight sun. Extremely popular, offering mountain and ocean views, it is only three kilometres from the base of Whalesafari and Andenes town. There is space for an unspecified number of touring units and you park where you like. With only 20 places with 16A electricity connections, it is advisable to arrive by mid-afternoon. Late arrivals may pitch and pay later when reception opens. Level areas of grass with some hardstanding can be found on gently sloping ground. Visitors come to Andenes for the opportunities to see whales at close quarters. Whalesafari is deemed the world's largest, most successful Arctic whale watching operation for the general public. It has an over 90 per cent 'chance of seeing the quarry' and a 'whale guarantee' that offers a free second chance or your money back if your first trip fails to locate a whale.

You might like to know

The village of Andenes is around 2 km. from the campsite and has a good range of amenities.

○ Environmental accreditation
☑ Reduced energy/water consumption policy
☑ Recycling and reusing policy
☑ Information about walking and cycling
☑ Footpaths within 500 m. of the site
○ Fishing within 1 km.
○ Riding or pony trekking within 1 km.
○ Direct river or lake access
○ Area of outstanding natural beauty or National Park within 10 km.
☑ Wildlife haven (on site or within 1 km)
○ Public transport
☑ Dogs welcome

Facilities: One building houses separate sex sanitary facilities, each providing two toilets, two showers (10 NOK) with curtain to keep clothes dry and three washbasins. In each, one toilet is suitable for disabled visitors and includes a washbasin. The reception building houses a well equipped kitchen, a large sitting/dining room, 2 showers, WC and washbasin. Laundry facilities. Motorcaravan service point. Chemical disposal (charged 30 NOK). Picnic tables. Swings for children. WiFi (free). Off site: Well stocked supermarket 250 m. On approach to town a garage, caravan dealer and another supermarket. From nearby village of Bleik (8 km), trips are available for deep sea fishing and to Bleiksøya, one of Norway's most famous bird cliffs with 80,000 pairs of puffins and 6,000 kittiwakes. Whalesafari 3 km. Guided walks. Kayaking.

Open: 1 June - 30 September.

Directions: Either take the scenic roads 946 and 947 on the west side of Andøy north or to the east road 82, site is on left 250 m. from where 947 rejoins the 82, 3 km. before Andenes. The scenic west route is 9 km. further.

GPS: 69.30411, 16.06641

Charges guide

Per pitch incl. electricity	NOK 200
tent pitch	NOK 100
car	NOK 100

Facilities: One heated toilet block provides washbasins, some in cubicles, and showers on payment. Family room with baby bath and changing mat, plus facilities for disabled visitors. Communal kitchen with cooking rings, small ovens, fridge and sinks (free hot water). Laundry facilities. Motorcaravan service point. Car wash facility. Barbecue area (covered). Playground. Duck pond. Fishing. Free WiFi over site. Old Trollveggen Station Master's apartment for hire by arrangement. Off site: Waymarked walks from site. Climbing, glacier walking and hiking. Fjord fishing. Sightseeing trips. The Troll Road. Mardalsfossen (waterfall). Geiranger and Åndalsnes.

Open: 10 May - 20 September.

Directions: Site is located on the E136 road, 10 km. south of Åndalsnes. It is signed.

GPS: 62.49444, 7.758333

Charges guide

Per unit incl. 2 persons and electricity	NOK 255
extra person (over 4 yrs)	NOK 15

Norway – Åndalsnes

Trollveggen Camping

Horgheimseidet, N-6300 Åndalsnes (Møre og Romsdal)
t: 71 22 37 00   e: post@trollveggen.no
alanrogers.com/NO2452 www.trollveggen.no

Accommodation: ☑ Pitch   ☑ Mobile home/chalet   ○ Hotel/B&B   ☑ Apartment

The location of this site provides a unique experience – it is set at the foot of the famous vertical cliff of Trollveggen (the Troll Wall), which is Europe's highest vertical mountain face. The site is pleasantly laid out in terraces with level grass pitches. The facility block, four cabins and reception are all very attractively built with grass roofs. Beside the river is an attractive barbecue area where barbecue parties are sometimes arranged. This site is a must for people who love nature. The site is surrounded by the Troll Peaks and the Romsdalshorn Mountains with the rapid river of Rauma flowing by. Close to Reinheimen (home of reindeer) National Park, and in the beautiful valley of Romsdalen you have the ideal starting point for trips to many outstanding attractions such as Trollstigen (The Troll Road) to Geiranger or to the Mardalsfossen waterfalls. In the mountains there are nature trails of various lengths and difficulties.

You might like to know

The Romsdal Alps area offers numerous hiking trails, many close to the site. Romsdalseggen, in particular, is a very popular hike, with wonderful views of the surrounding mountains and the Romsdal valley.

○ Environmental accreditation
○ Reduced energy/water consumption policy
○ Recycling and reusing policy
☑ Information about walking and cycling
☑ Footpaths within 500 m. of the site
○ Fishing within 1 km.
○ Riding or pony trekking within 1 km.
☑ Direct river or lake access
☑ Area of outstanding natural beauty or National Park within 10 km.
☑ Wildlife haven (on site or within 1 km)
○ Public transport
☑ Dogs welcome

Facilities: Central unisex sanitary block has open washbasins and hot showers, a large well equipped kitchen, dining area with TV, small laundry, large drying room and several lounge areas. Additional smaller separate sex sanitary blocks each have WC, shower and enclosed washbasin. Kitchen. Fish preparation and freezing areas. Motorcaravan services. Sauna. Satellite TV. Motor boat hire. Free bicycle hire. Free WiFi. Organised sea fishing and sightseeing trips in owner's sea-going boat. Sales of fresh fish and prepared fish dishes for guests to heat. Off site: Golf 6 km.

Open: All year.

Directions: Site is on the little island of Ekkilsøya which is reached via a side road running west from the main Rv 64 road, 1.5 km. south of Bremsnes.

GPS: 63.08114, 7.59569

Charges guide

Per unit incl. 2 persons and electricity	NOK 153 - 200
extra person	NOK 30
child	NOK 20
dog	no charge

No credit cards.

Skjerneset Bryggecamping

Ekkilsoya, N-6530 Averoy (Møre og Romsdal)
t: 71 51 18 94 e: info@skjerneset.com
alanrogers.com/NO2490 www.skjerneset.com

Accommodation: ☑ Pitch ☑ Mobile home/chalet ○ Hotel/B&B ☑ Apartment

Uniquely centred around a working fishing quay set in an idyllic bay, Skjerneset Camping has been developed by the Otterlei family to give visitors an historical insight into this industry. It steps back in time in all but its facilities and offers 25 boats to hire and organised trips on a real fishing boat. Found on the tiny island of Ekkilsøya off Averøy, there is space for 30 caravans or motorcaravans on gravel hardstandings landscaped into rocks and trees, each individually shaped and sized and all having electricity connections (10/16A). There are grassy areas for tents on the upper terraces and six fully equipped cabins. Although the fishing industry here has declined, it is still the dominant activity. The old Klippfisk warehouse is now a fascinating 'fisherimuseum' and also houses the main sanitary installations and reception. It encompasses a large kitchen, laundry, several lounges with satellite TV and five small four-bed apartments.

You might like to know

Why not try some relaxing fishing? The campsite will be happy to arrange a boat for you.

- ○ Environmental accreditation
- ☑ Reduced energy/water consumption policy
- ☑ Recycling and reusing policy
- ☑ Information about walking and cycling
- ☑ Footpaths within 500 m. of the site
- ☑ Fishing within 1 km.
- ○ Riding or pony trekking within 1 km.
- ○ Direct river or lake access
- ○ Area of outstanding natural beauty or National Park within 10 km.
- ☑ Wildlife haven (on site or within 1 km)
- ○ Public transport
- ☑ Dogs welcome

Facilities: Three modern, heated sanitary blocks have showers (on payment), en-suite family rooms, washing up facilities and kitchen. Facilities for disabled campers in one block. Motorcaravan services. Restaurant and takeaway (15/6-15/8). Shop (1/5-1/10). Playground. Lake swimming, boating and fishing. Trampoline. Bouncy cushion. Outdoor fitness. Beach volleyball. Barbecue area and hot tub (winter). Boat, canoe and pedalo hire. Elk safaris arranged. Climbing, rafting and canoeing courses arranged (linked with Trollaktiv). Cross-country skiing (winter). Car wash. Free WiFi. Off site: Rock climbing wall. Marked forest trails. Mineral centres and mines.

Open: All year.

Directions: Site is on route 9, 2.5 km. north of the town of Byglandsfjord on the eastern shores of the lake.

GPS: 58.68839, 7.80175

Charges guide

Per unit incl. 2 persons and electricity NOK	245 - 275
extra person NOK	10
child (5-12 yrs) NOK	5
dog	no charge

Neset Camping

N-4741 Byglandsfjord (Aust-Agder)
t: 37 93 42 55   e: post@neset.no
alanrogers.com/NO2610   www.neset.no

Accommodation: ☑ Pitch   ☑ Mobile home/chalet   ○ Hotel/B&B   ○ Apartment

On a semi-promontory on the shores of the 40 km. long Byglandsfjord, Neset is a well run, friendly site ideal for spending a few active days, or as a short stop en route north from the ferry port of Kristiansand (from England or Denmark). Neset is situated on well kept grassy meadows by the lake shore, with water on three sides and the road on the fourth. There are 260 unmarked pitches with electricity and cable TV, and 40 hardstandings for motorcaravans. The main building houses reception, a small shop and a restaurant with fine views over the water. The campsite has a range of activities to keep you busy, and the excellent hardstandings for motorcaravans look out onto the lake. Byglandsfjord offers good fishing (mainly trout) and the area has marked trails for cycling, riding or walking in an area famous for its minerals. Samples of these can be found in reception, and day trips to specialist exhibitions at the Mineralparken (8 km) are possible.

You might like to know

Mountaineering courses are available. You can also go in search of various minerals along the Evje Mineral Path.

- ○ Environmental accreditation
- ○ Reduced energy/water consumption policy
- ○ Recycling and reusing policy
- ☑ Information about walking and cycling
- ☑ Footpaths within 500 m. of the site
- ☑ Fishing within 1 km.
- ○ Riding or pony trekking within 1 km.
- ☑ Direct river or lake access
- ○ Area of outstanding natural beauty or National Park within 10 km.
- ○ Wildlife haven (on site or within 1 km)
- ○ Public transport
- ☑ Dogs welcome

Facilities: Four modern, very clean and well equipped toilet blocks are built in traditional Portuguese style with hot water throughout. Washing machines. Motorcaravan services. Bar and restaurant (1/4-30/9). Shop (all year, bread to order). Lounge. Playground. Fishing. Boat hire. Tennis. Riding. Medical post. Car wash. Dogs are not accepted in July/Aug. Facilities and amenities may be reduced outside the main season. Off site: Swimming and boating in the lake.

Open: All year.

Directions: From A2 between Setubal and the Algarve take exit 10 on IP8 (Ferreira and Beja). Take road to Torrao and 13 km. later, 1 km. north of Odivelas, turn right towards Barragem and site is 3 km. after crossing head of reservoir following small signs.

GPS: 38.1812, -8.10293

Charges guide

Per unit incl. 2 persons and electricity	€ 27,00
extra person	€ 6,00
child (5-10 yrs)	€ 3,00

No credit cards.

Camping Markádia

Barragem de Odivelas, Apdo 17, P-7920-999 Alvito (Beja)
t: 284 763 141 e: markadia@hotmail.com
alanrogers.com/PO8350 www.markadia.net

Accommodation: ☑ Pitch ○ Mobile home/chalet ○ Hotel/B&B ○ Apartment

A tranquil, lakeside site in an unspoilt setting, this will appeal most to those nature lovers who want to 'get away from it all' and to those who enjoy country pursuits such as walking, fishing and riding. There are 130 casual unmarked pitches on undulating grass and sand with ample electricity connections (16A). The site is lit but a torch is required. The friendly Dutch owner has carefully planned the site so each pitch has its own oak tree to provide shade. The open countryside and lake provide excellent views and a very pleasant environment. The lake is in fact a 1,000-hectare reservoir, and more than 150 species of birds can be found in the area. The stellar views in the very low ambient lighting are wonderful at night. The bar/restaurant with a terrace is open daily in season but weekends only during the winter. One can swim in the reservoir, and canoes, pedaloes and windsurfers are available for hire.

You might like to know

Dogs are welcome on site from September to June, but not in peak season.

- ○ Environmental accreditation
- ☑ Reduced energy/water consumption policy
- ☑ Recycling and reusing policy
- ☑ Information about walking and cycling
- ☑ Footpaths within 500 m. of the site
- ☑ Fishing within 1 km.
- ☑ Riding or pony trekking within 1 km.
- ☑ Direct river or lake access
- ☑ Area of outstanding natural beauty or National Park within 10 km.
- ○ Wildlife haven (on site or within 1 km)
- ○ Public transport
- ☑ Dogs welcome

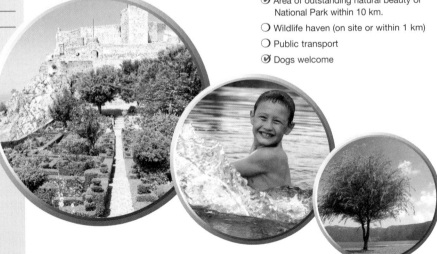

Facilities: Three very clean sanitary blocks provide mixed style WCs, controllable showers and hot water. Good facilities for disabled visitors. Laundry. Gas supplies. Shop. Restaurant/bar. Outdoor pool (June-Sept). Playground. TV room (satellite). Medical post. Good tennis courts. Minigolf. Adventure park. Car wash. Barbecue areas. Torches useful. English spoken. Attractive bungalows to rent. WiFi in reception/bar area. Off site: Fishing, riding and bicycle hire 800 m.

Open: All year.

Directions: From north, N103 (Braga-Chaves), turn left at N205 (7.5 km. north of Braga). Follow N205 to Caldelas Terras de Bouro and Covide where site is signed to Campo do Gerês. An eastern approach from N103 is for the adventurous but with magnificent views over mountains and lakes.

GPS: 41.7631, -8.1905

Charges guide

Per unit incl. 2 persons and electricity	€ 13,60 - € 28,60
extra person	€ 3,20 - € 5,50
child (5-11 yrs)	€ 2,00 - € 3,30
dog	€ 1,50 - € 3,00

Parque de Campismo de Cerdeira

Rua de Cerdeira 400, P-4840 030 Campo do Gerês (Braga)
t: 253 351 005   e: info@parquecerdeira.com
alanrogers.com/PO8370   www.parquecerdeira.com

Accommodation: ☑ Pitch ☑ Mobile home/chalet ○ Hotel/B&B ○ Apartment

Located in the Peneda-Gerês National Park, amidst spectacular mountain scenery, this excellent site offers modern facilities in a truly natural area. The national park is home to all manner of flora, fauna and wildlife, including the roebuck, wolf and wild boar. The well fenced, professional and peaceful site offers 600 good sized, unmarked, mostly level, grassy pitches in a shady woodland setting. Electricity (5/10A) is available for 200 of the 550 touring pitches, though some long leads may be required. A very large timber complex, tastefully designed with the use of noble materials – granite and wood – provides a superb restaurant with a comprehensive menu. A pool with a separated section for toddlers is a welcome, cooling relief in the height of summer. There are unlimited opportunities in the immediate area for fishing, riding, canoeing, mountain biking and climbing, so take advantage of this quality mountain hospitality.

You might like to know

Nature lovers will be in their element in the Peneda-Gerês National Park, a haven for wildlife, including the wolf and royal eagle. Human occupation dates back 7,000 years and ancient artefacts are frequently found.

- ☑ Environmental accreditation
- ☑ Reduced energy/water consumption policy
- ☑ Recycling and reusing policy
- ☑ Information about walking and cycling
- ○ Footpaths within 500 m. of the site
- ☑ Fishing within 1 km.
- ☑ Riding or pony trekking within 1 km.
- ○ Direct river or lake access
- ○ Area of outstanding natural beauty or National Park within 10 km.
- ☑ Wildlife haven (on site or within 1 km)
- ○ Public transport
- ☑ Dogs welcome

Facilities: The single rustic sanitary building has British style WCs with hot showers and pairs of washbasins in cubicles (cold water only). Washing machine. No facilities for disabled campers. Baker calls daily. Rustic room serves as reception and lounge with library and small kitchen and self-service bar (tea, coffee, soft drinks, bottled beer, wine). Swimming pool with terrace. WiFi in upper part of site (free). Three apartments to rent. Off site: Town with shops, bars and restaurants and bus service 1 km. Fishing, swimming and watersports 6 km. Tomar 19 km.

Open: 1 March - 15 October.

Directions: Ferreira do Zêzere is 64 km south of Coimbra. From Lisbon on A1 north take exit 7 onto A23 (Abrantes) then head north on A13 (Tomar) and northeast on N238 to Ferreira do Zêzere. Take N348 (Vila de Rei) and site is signed to left 1 km. from town (do not enter town). From north on A1 south of Coimbra take new A13-1 and A13 (Tomar). At exit 21 take N348 to Ferreira and then as above.

GPS: 39.70075, -8.2782

Charges guide

Per unit incl. 2 persons and electricity	€ 17,50 - € 21,05
extra person	€ 3,50 - € 4,50
child (under 11 yrs)	€ 1,75 - € 2,25

Camping Quinta da Cerejeira

Rua D. Maria Fernanda da Mota Cardoso 902, P-2240-333 Ferreira do Zêzere (Santarem)
t: 249 361 756 e: info@cerejeira.com
alanrogers.com/PO8550 www.cerejeira.com

Accommodation: ☑ Pitch ○ Mobile home/chalet ○ Hotel/B&B ☑ Apartment

This is a delightful, small, family-owned venture run by Gert and Teunie Verheij. It is a converted farm (quinta) which has been coaxed into a very special campsite. You pitch where you choose under fruit and olive trees on gently-sloping grass below the house or on terraces beyond. There is space for 25 units with 18 electrical connections (6A). It is very peaceful with views of the surrounding green hills from the charming vine-covered patio above a small swimming pool. A visit to Tomar to explore the temple and legends of the Knights Templar is highly recommended. Nearby Ferreira do Zêzere has shops, bars and restaurants, whilst Tomar offers a wider choice along with its numerous historical and architectural sights. Reception has information about walks in the surrounding countryside and drives to numerous interesting sites in the area, including the Sanctuary at Fátima and the Monastery at Alcobaça.

You might like to know

The surroundings of Quinta da Cerejeira are perfect for both short and longer walks. The green hills contrast with the pretty, white villages and farms. One of Europe's largest reservoirs can be reached on foot.

○ Environmental accreditation
☑ Reduced energy/water consumption policy
☑ Recycling and reusing policy
☑ Information about walking and cycling
☑ Footpaths within 500 m. of the site
☑ Fishing within 1 km.
○ Riding or pony trekking within 1 km.
○ Direct river or lake access
○ Area of outstanding natural beauty or National Park within 10 km.
○ Wildlife haven (on site or within 1 km)
○ Public transport
○ Dogs welcome

Facilities:
Facilities: The modern toilet block has British style toilets, open washbasins and controllable hot showers (free). It could be pressed in high season and hot water to the showers is only available from 07.00-10.00 and from 19.00-22.00. Shop for basics. Bar and lakeside bar. Small restaurant. Basic playground (new playground planned). Pedalo, canoe and rowing boat hire. Water skiing. Fishing (with permit). Torch useful. Off site: Slanica Island.

Open: May - September.

Directions: From Ruzomberok take E77 road north towards Trstena. Turn left in Tvrdosin on the 520 road towards Námestovo. Site is on the right.

GPS: 49.359333, 19.555

Charges guide

Per unit incl. 2 persons and electricity € 13,50 - € 14,00	
extra person € 3,00	
child (4-10 yrs) € 1,50	
dog € 1,50	

Autocamping Stara Hora

Oravska Priehrada, SK-02901 Namestovo (Zilina)
t: 043 552 2223 e: camp.s.hora@mail.t-com.sk
alanrogers.com/SK4905 www.oravskapriehrada.sk

Accommodation: ☑ Pitch ☑ Mobile home/chalet ○ Hotel/B&B ○ Apartment

Stara Hora has a beautiful location on the Orava artificial lake. It is in the northeast of Slovakia in the Tatra Mountains and attracts visitors from all over Europe which creates a happy and sometimes noisy atmosphere. The site has its own pebble beach with a large grass area behind it for sunbathing. Autocamping Stara Hora is on steeply sloping ground with 160 grassy pitches, all for touring units and with 10A electricity. The lower pitches are level and have good views over the lake, pitches at the top are mainly used by tents. The lake provides opportunities for fishing, boating and sailing and the area is good for hiking and cycling and in winter, it is a popular skiing area.

You might like to know

Stara Hora is located in a beautiful natural setting on the banks of the Orava reservoir. There are some excellent walking opportunities, including the area's highest peak, Oravské Beskids.

- ○ Environmental accreditation
- ☑ Reduced energy/water consumption policy
- ☑ Recycling and reusing policy
- ☑ Information about walking and cycling
- ☑ Footpaths within 500 m. of the site
- ☑ Fishing within 1 km.
- ○ Riding or pony trekking within 1 km.
- ☑ Direct river or lake access
- ☑ Area of outstanding natural beauty or National Park within 10 km.
- ○ Wildlife haven (on site or within 1 km)
- ○ Public transport
- ○ Dogs welcome

Facilities: One modern toilet block with controllable showers. WC only for disabled visitors. Laundry with sinks. Bar/restaurant. Play area. Fishing (permit required). Torch useful. WiFi. Off site: Riding 500 m. Bicycle hire 10 km. Rambling. Rafting. Paragliding.

Open: April - October.

Directions: Site is on the main Kranjska Gora-Bovec road and is well signed 3 km. east of Soca. Access is via a sharp right turn from the main road and over a small bridge and right again. The road is winding in places with a moderate descent. GPS use co-ordinates.

GPS: 46.33007, 13.644

Charges guide

Per unit incl. 2 persons
and electricity € 23,00 - € 27,00

extra person € 11,50 - € 13,50

child (7-12 yrs) € 6,00 - € 7,00

dog no charge

Slovenia – Soca

Kamp Klin

Lepena 1, SLO-5232 Soca (Slovenia)
t: 053 889 513 e: kampklin@siol.net
alanrogers.com/SV4235

Accommodation: ☑ Pitch ☑ Mobile home/chalet ○ Hotel/B&B ○ Apartment

With an attractive location surrounded by mountains in the Triglav National Park, Kamp Klin is next to the confluence of the Soca and Lepenca rivers, which makes it an ideal base for fishing, kayaking and rafting. The campsite has 50 pitches, all for tourers, 50 with 7A electricity, on one large, grassy field, connected by a circular, gravel access road. It is attractively landscaped with flowers and young trees, which provide some shade. Some pitches are right on the bank of the river (unfenced) and there are beautiful views of the river and the mountains. Kamp Klin is privately owned and there is a 'pension' next door, all run by the Zorc family, who serve local dishes with compe (potatoes), cottage cheese, grilled trout and local salami in the restaurant. From the site, one can drive to a parking place and explore the Triglav mountain and its beautiful viewpoint with marked walking routes. Like so many Slovenian sites in this area, this is a good holiday base for the active camper.

You might like to know

Kamp Klin is near the world famous Kanin Plateau. The restaurant serves trout freshly caught from the river.

- ☑ Environmental accreditation
- ☑ Reduced energy/water consumption policy
- ☑ Recycling and reusing policy
- ☑ Information about walking and cycling
- ☑ Footpaths within 500 m. of the site
- ☑ Fishing within 1 km.
- ☑ Riding or pony trekking within 1 km.
- ☑ Direct river or lake access
- ☑ Area of outstanding natural beauty or National Park within 10 km.
- ○ Wildlife haven (on site or within 1 km)
- ○ Public transport
- ☑ Dogs welcome

Facilities: Two attractive and well maintained log-built toilet blocks, both recently renovated. Facilities for disabled visitors. Laundry facilities. Motorcaravan services. Shop (March-Nov). Café serves light meals, snacks and drinks apparently with flexible closing hours. Play area. Bowling. Fishing. Bicycle hire. Canoe hire. Climbing walls. Communal barbecue. WiFi. Off site: Town within walking distance. Riding 5 km. Golf 15 km. Trilav National Park. Guided tours in the Soca valley and around Slovenia start from the campsite.

Open: All year.

Directions: Approaching Kobarid from Tolmin on 102, just before Kobarid turn right on 203 towards Bovec and after 100 m. take descending slip road to right and keep more or less straight on to Napoléon's bridge (c. 500 m). Cross bridge and site is on left in 100 m.

GPS: 46.25075, 13.58658

Charges guide

Per unit incl. 2 persons and electricity	€ 25,00 - € 28,00
extra person	€ 10,50 - € 12,00
child (7-12 yrs)	€ 5,25 - € 6,00
dog	€ 2,00

Slovenia – Kobarid

Kamp Koren Kobarid

Ladra 1b, SLO-5222 Kobarid (Slovenia)
t: 053 891 311 e: info@kamp-koren.si
alanrogers.com/SV4270 www.kamp-koren.si

Accommodation: ☑ Pitch ☑ Mobile home/chalet ○ Hotel/B&B ○ Apartment

Kamp Koren, Slovenia's first ecological site, is in a quiet location above the Soca river gorge, within easy walking distance of Kobarid. The site has 90 slightly sloping pitches, all with 6/16A electricity and ample tree shade. It is deservedly very popular with those interested in outdoor sports, be it on the water, in the mountains or in the air. At the same time, its peaceful situation makes it an ideal choice for those seeking a relaxing break. There are six well equipped chalets, and a shady area for mainly tents was opened in 2014 at the top of the site. Kobarid, probably best approached via Udine in Italy, is a pleasant country town, with easy access to nearby rivers, valleys and mountains, which alone justify a visit to Kamp Koren. But most British visitors will remember it for the opportunity it provides to fill that curious gap in their knowledge of European history. The local museum in Kobarid was recently voted European Museum of the Year and is excellent.

You might like to know

Kamp Koren was the first site in Slovenia (in 2011) to meet the criteria for the European Ecolabel, certifying its environmentally friendly status.

- ☑ Environmental accreditation
- ☑ Reduced energy/water consumption policy
- ☑ Recycling and reusing policy
- ☑ Information about walking and cycling
- ☑ Footpaths within 500 m. of the site
- ☑ Fishing within 1 km.
- ☑ Riding or pony trekking within 1 km.
- ☑ Direct river or lake access
- ☑ Area of outstanding natural beauty or National Park within 10 km.
- ○ Wildlife haven (on site or within 1 km)
- ○ Public transport
- ☑ Dogs welcome

Facilities: Two toilet blocks (one new) have modern fittings with toilets, open plan washbasins and controllable hot showers. Motorcaravan service point. Bar/restaurant with open-air terrace (evenings only) and open-air kitchen. Sauna. Playing field. Play area. Fishing. Mountain bike hire. Russian bowling. Excursions (52). Live music and gatherings around the camp fire. Indian village. Hostel. Skiing in winter. Kayaking. Mobile homes to rent. Climbing wall. Rafting. Off site: Fishing 2 km. Recica and other villages with much culture and folklore are close. Indian sauna at Coze.

Open: All year.

Directions: From Ljubljana/Celje autobahn A1. Exit at Sentupert and turn north towards Mozirje (14 km). At roundabout just before Mozirje, hard left staying on the 225 for 6 km. to Nizka then just after the circular automatic petrol station, left where site is signed.

GPS: 46.31168, 14.90913

Charges guide

Per unit incl. 2 persons and electricity	€ 17,80 - € 23,00
extra person	€ 7,50 - € 10,00
child (5-15 yrs)	€ 3,50 - € 6,00
dog	€ 2,50 - € 3,00

Camping Menina

Varpolje 105, SLO-3332 Recica ob Savinji (Slovenia)
t: 035 835 027   e: info@campingmenina.com
alanrogers.com/SV4405   www.campingmenina.com

Accommodation: ✔ Pitch   ✔ Mobile home/chalet   ○ Hotel/B&B   ✔ Apartment

Camping Menina is in the heart of the 35 km. long Upper Savinja Valley, surrounded by 2,500 m. high mountains and unspoilt nature. It is being improved every year by the young, enthusiastic owner, Jurij Kolenc and has 200 pitches, all for touring units, on grassy fields under mature trees and with access from gravel roads. All have 6-10A electricity. The Savinja river runs along one side of the site, but if its water is too cold for swimming, the site also has a lake which can be used for swimming. This site is a perfect base for walking or mountain biking in the mountains. A wealth of maps and routes are available from reception. Rafting, canyoning and kayaking, and visits to a fitness studio, sauna and massage salon are organised. The site is now open all year to offer skiing holidays.

You might like to know

Mozirski Gaj (4 km) is a beautiful botanical park with an open-air ethnographic museum.

- ✔ Environmental accreditation
- ○ Reduced energy/water consumption policy
- ✔ Recycling and reusing policy
- ✔ Information about walking and cycling
- ✔ Footpaths within 500 m. of the site
- ✔ Fishing within 1 km.
- ○ Riding or pony trekking within 1 km.
- ✔ Direct river or lake access
- ✔ Area of outstanding natural beauty or National Park within 10 km.
- ○ Wildlife haven (on site or within 1 km)
- ○ Public transport
- ✔ Dogs welcome

Röstånga Camping & Bad

Blinkarpsvägen 3, S-268 68 Röstånga (Skåne Län)
t: 043 591 064   e: nystrand@msn.com
alanrogers.com/SW2630 www.rostangacamping.se

Accommodation: ☑ Pitch ☑ Mobile home/chalet ○ Hotel/B&B ○ Apartment

Facilities: Four good, heated sanitary blocks with free hot water and facilities for babies and disabled visitors. Motorcaravan service point. Laundry with washing machines and dryers. Kitchen with cooking rings, oven and microwave. Small shop at reception. Bar, restaurant and takeaway. Minigolf. Tennis. Fitness trail. Fishing. Canoe hire. Children's club. WiFi (free). Off site: Swimming pool complex adjacent to site (free for campers as is a visit to the zoo). Golf 11 km. Motor racing track at Ring Knutstorp 8 km.

Open: 17 April - 20 September.

Directions: From Malmö: drive towards Lund and follow road no. 108 to Röstånga. From Stockholm: turn off at Östra Ljungby and take road no. 13 to Röstånga. In Röstånga drive through the village on road no. 108 and follow the signs.

GPS: 55.996583, 13.28005

Charges guide

Per unit incl. 2 persons
and electricity € 25,00 - € 33,00

No credit cards.

Beside the Söderåsen National Park, this scenic campsite has its own fishing lake and many activities for the whole family. There are 180 large, level, grassy pitches with electricity (10A) and a quiet area for tents with a view over the fishing lake. The tent area has its own service building and several barbecue places. A large holiday home and 21 pleasant cabins are available to rent all year round. A pool complex adjacent to the site provides a 50 m. swimming pool, three children's pools and a water slide, all heated during peak season. Activities are arranged on the site in high season, including a children's club with exciting activities such as treasure hunts and gold panning, and for adults, aquarobics, Nordic walking and tennis. The Söderåsen National Park offers hiking and bicycle trails. The friendly staff will be happy to help you to plan interesting excursions in the area.

You might like to know

Located on the southern slope of Söderasen National Park, one of Sweden's most visited tourist attractions, which has its own unique beauty and an abundance of flora and fauna.

○ Environmental accreditation
☑ Reduced energy/water consumption policy
☑ Recycling and reusing policy
☑ Information about walking and cycling
○ Footpaths within 500 m. of the site
☑ Fishing within 1 km.
○ Riding or pony trekking within 1 km.
☑ Direct river or lake access
☑ Area of outstanding natural beauty or
     National Park within 10 km.
☑ Wildlife haven (on site or within 1 km)
○ Public transport
○ Dogs welcome

Facilities: The original sanitary block near reception is supplemented by one in the wooded area, both refurbished. Hot showers in cubicles with communal changing area are free. Separate saunas for each sex and facilities for disabled visitors and babies. Campers' kitchen at each block with cooking, dishwashing and laundry facilities. Small, but well stocked shop. Very good angling shop. Fully licensed restaurant with takeaway. Playground. Minigolf. Lake swimming. Fishing. Boules. Off site: The town of Tidaholm and Lake Hornborga. Fishing 2 km. Riding 10 km. Bicycle hire 15 km.

Open: All year (full services 20/6-11/8).

Directions: Approach site from no. 195 road at Brandstorp, 40 km. north of Jönköping, turn west at petrol station and camp sign signed Hökensås. Site is 9 km. up this road.

GPS: 58.0982, 14.0746

Charges guide

Per unit incl. 2 persons and electricity € 24,70

Hökensås Camping & Holiday Village

Blåhult, S-522 91 Tidaholm (Västra Götalands Län)
t: 050 223 053 e: info@hokensas.nu
alanrogers.com/SW2720 www.hokensas.nordiccamping.se/en

Accommodation: ☑ Pitch ☑ Mobile home/chalet ○ Hotel/B&B ○ Apartment

Hökensås is located just west of Lake Vättern and south of Tidaholm, in a beautiful nature reserve of wild, unspoiled scenery. This pleasant campsite is part of a holiday complex that includes wooden cabins for rent. It is relaxed and informal, with over 200 pitches either under trees or on a more open area at the far end, divided into rows by wooden rails. These are numbered and electricity (10A) is available on 135. Tents can go on the large grassy open areas by reception. This site is a find for all kinds of people who enjoy outdoor activities. The park is based on a 100 km. ridge, a glacier area with many impressive boulders and ice age debris but now thickly forested with majestic pines and silver birches, with a small, brilliant lake at every corner. The forests and lakes provide wonderful opportunities for walking, cycling (gravel tracks and marked walks) a real paradise for anglers, swimming and when the snow falls, winter sports.

You might like to know

Hökensås Nature reserve is adjacent to the site, and is home to some popular hiking tracks that pass through beautiful, woodland scenery. In winter, these tracks become delightful Nordic skiing routes.

○ Environmental accreditation
☑ Reduced energy/water consumption policy
☑ Recycling and reusing policy
☑ Information about walking and cycling
☑ Footpaths within 500 m. of the site
☑ Fishing within 1 km.
○ Riding or pony trekking within 1 km.
☑ Direct river or lake access
☑ Area of outstanding natural beauty or National Park within 10 km.
○ Wildlife haven (on site or within 1 km)
○ Public transport
○ Dogs welcome

Facilities: The main toilet block has hot showers (on payment), washbasins in cubicles, WCs and a hairdressing cubicle. With a further small block at the top of the site, the provision should be adequate. Facilities for disabled visitors. Laundry with drying rooms for bad weather. Cooking rooms for tenters. Restaurant (high season). Shop. Minigolf. Playground. Lake for swimming, fishing and boating. Off site: Dalslands Aktiviteter, Dalslands kanal.

Open: All year (full services 22/6-15/8).

Directions: From Åmål take road no. 164 towards Bengtfors, then 172 towards Billingsfors and Dals Långed. Site is signed 5 km. south of Billingsfors, 1 km. down a good road. From the south, (Uddevalla) take road 172.

GPS: 58.95296, 12.25242

Charges guide

Per pitch incl. electricity SEK 200 - 280

Sweden – Dals Långed

Laxsjöns Camping och Friluftsgård

S-660 10 Dals Långed (Västra Götalands Län)
t: 053 130 010   e: office@laxsjon.se
alanrogers.com/SW2740 www.laxsjon.se

Accommodation: ☑ Pitch ☑ Mobile home/chalet ☑ Hotel/B&B ○ Apartment

In the beautiful Dalsland region, Laxsjöns is an all-year-round site, catering for winter sports enthusiasts as well as summer tourists and groups. On the shores of the lake, the site is in two main areas – one flat, near the entrance, with hardstandings and the other on attractive, sloping, grassy areas adjoining. In all, there are 180 places for caravans and motorcaravans, 150 with electricity (10/16A), plus more for tents. Leisure facilities on the site include minigolf, trampolines and a playground. A restaurant is at the top of the site with a good range of dishes in high season. In addition, there is a lake for swimming, fishing and canoeing (boats available). The site is located in the centre of Dalsland, west of Lake Vänern, in an area of deep forests, endless lakes and river valleys, and is one of the loveliest and most interesting regions in this always peaceful and scenic country.

You might like to know

Canoes and boats (with or without motors) are available for rent on the lake – an ideal way to explore Dalsland.

○ Environmental accreditation
☑ Reduced energy/water consumption policy
☑ Recycling and reusing policy
☑ Information about walking and cycling
☑ Footpaths within 500 m. of the site
☑ Fishing within 1 km.
○ Riding or pony trekking within 1 km.
☑ Direct river or lake access
☑ Area of outstanding natural beauty or National Park within 10 km.
○ Wildlife haven (on site or within 1 km)
○ Public transport
○ Dogs welcome

Facilities: A smart new pine clad toilet block, with a separate provision of four family-sized showers, with solar heated rainwater. Washing machine and dryer. Small fridge and freezer. Home produced lamb, burgers and sausages available. Facilities for field studies and opportunities for educational groups and schools to learn about the local environment. Bush craft days. Arts workshops. Fishing (requires an EA rod licence and tokens available from the West Country Rivers Trust). Dogs are not accepted. Off site: Riding and cycling 1 mile. Pubs 1.5 and 2.5 miles. Beach 16 km. Sustrans Route 3 passes close by. North and south coasts within easy reach.

Open: 1 April - 31 October.

Directions: On A30 Bodmin Moor pass Jamaica Inn and sign for Colliford Lake and watch for St Breward sign (to right) immediately at end of dual carriageway. Follow narrow road over moor for 2 miles ignoring any turns, including right turn to St Breward just before South Penquite sign. Follow track over stone bridge through farm gate, then bear left to camping fields. Book in at Farm House.
GPS: 50.5445, -4.671833

Charges guide

Per person	£ 8.00
child (5-15 yrs)	£ 4.00

No credit cards.

South Penquite Farm

South Penquite, Blisland, Bodmin PL30 4LH (Cornwall)
t: 01208 850491   e: thefarm@bodminmoor.co.uk
alanrogers.com/UK0302 www.southpenquite.co.uk

Accommodation: ☑ Pitch ☑ Mobile home/chalet ○ Hotel/B&B ○ Apartment

South Penquite offers real camping with no frills. It is set on a 200-hectare hill farm, high on Bodmin Moor between the villages of Blisland and Saint Breward. The farm achieved organic status in 2001 and runs a flock of 100 ewes and a herd of 20 cattle and horses. The camping is small scale and intended to have a low impact on the surrounding environment. Fifty tents or simple motorcaravans (no caravans) can pitch around the edge of three walled fields, roughly cut in the midst of the moor. You can find shelter or a view. Four yurts are available to rent in one field, complete with wood burning stoves – quite original. Campfires are permitted with wood available from the farmhouse. You will also find horses, ponies, chickens, geese, ducks and turkeys which show their approval (or not) by the skin on their necks changing colour! A two-mile walk takes you over most of the farm and some of the moor, via a Bronze Age hut settlement, the river and a standing stone.

You might like to know

There are opportunities to study a variety of subjects, from butterflies to archaeology!

○ Environmental accreditation
☑ Reduced energy/water consumption policy
☑ Recycling and reusing policy
☑ Information about walking and cycling
☑ Footpaths within 500 m. of the site
☑ Fishing within 1 km.
☑ Riding or pony trekking within 1 km.
☑ Direct river or lake access
○ Area of outstanding natural beauty or National Park within 10 km.
☑ Wildlife haven (on site or within 1 km)
○ Public transport
○ Dogs welcome

Facilities: Five toilet blocks are fully equipped and include laundry facilities. The newest block (in field 5) has under-floor heating. Facilities for disabled visitors and private family washrooms beside reception. Well stocked shop. Takeaway with restaurant and bars (April-Oct). Entertainment (high season). Indoor pool (heated Easter-Oct, charged). Riding. 18-hole pitch and putt. Crazy golf. 'Kiddies kar' track (all charged). Games room. Play area. Organised games and activities (high season). WiFi on part of site. ATM. Woodland walks. Off site: Fishing and boat launching 4 miles. Bicycle hire 10 miles.

Open: All year.

Directions: From Barnstaple take A39 towards Lynton. After 1 mile turn left (B3230). Turn right at garage on A3123. Park is 1.5 miles on right.

GPS: 51.16498, -4.05995

Charges guide

Per unit incl. 2 persons
and electricity £ 10.45 - £ 27.50

extra person no charge - £ 4.70

child (5-12 yrs) no charge - £ 2.60

dog £ 1.70 - £ 2.70

Stowford Farm Meadows

Berry Down, Combe Martin, Ilfracombe EX34 0PW (Devon)
t: 01271 882476   e: enquiries@stowford.co.uk
alanrogers.com/UK0690 www.stowford.co.uk

Accommodation: ☑ Pitch ☑ Mobile home/chalet ○ Hotel/B&B ○ Apartment

Stowford Farm is a very large, friendly, family run park set in 500 acres of the rolling North Devon countryside, good for recreation and walking and within easy reach of five local beaches. The touring park and its facilities have been developed in the fields and farm buildings surrounding the attractive old farmhouse and provide a village-like centre with a comfortable, spacious feel. There are 710 marked pitches, separated by beech and ash hedges, on five slightly sloping meadows. Most have 10/16A electricity, nine are on hardstanding and all are accessed by hard roads. Stowford also provides plenty to keep the whole family occupied without leaving the park, including woodland walks and horse riding from the park's own stables. The Old Stable Bar offers entertainment in high season including barn dances, discos, karaoke and other musical evenings.

You might like to know

Three and a half miles of marked nature walks start and finish on the campsite. The 70 acres of woodland is home to deer, badgers, squirrels and buzzards.

- ☑ Environmental accreditation
- ○ Reduced energy/water consumption policy
- ○ Recycling and reusing policy
- ☑ Information about walking and cycling
- ☑ Footpaths within 500 m. of the site
- ○ Fishing within 1 km.
- ☑ Riding or pony trekking within 1 km.
- ○ Direct river or lake access
- ☑ Area of outstanding natural beauty or National Park within 10 km.
- ☑ Wildlife haven (on site or within 1 km)
- ○ Public transport
- ☑ Dogs welcome

Facilities: Three toilet blocks include facilities for disabled visitors, a baby room and laundry facilities. Gas. Well stocked shop, bar, restaurant and takeaway (all season). Indoor leisure centre with pool, gym, etc. with trained staff (membership on either daily or weekly basis). Outdoor heated pool (25/5-5/9). Adventure play area. Tennis. Fishing. Bicycle hire. Entertainment programme. Special environmental Acorn activities for the family. WiFi (charged). Torches useful. Off site: The Norfolk coast, Felbrigg Hall, the Walsingham Shrine and the Norfolk Broads National Park are nearby. Many bird and nature reserves.

Open: 10 February - 2 January.

Directions: On A148 road from Holt to Cromer, after High Kelling, turn left just before Bodham village (international sign) signed Weybourne. Follow road for 1 mile to park.

GPS: 52.92880, 1.14953

Charges guide

Per unit incl. electricity £ 18.65 - £ 33.85	
with full services £ 24.30 - £ 41.95	
dog (max. 2) £ 3.15 - £ 5.20	
awning £ 2.15 - £ 5.20	

United Kingdom – Sheringham

Kelling Heath Holiday Park

Weybourne, Holt, Sheringham NR25 7HW (Norfolk)
t: 01263 588181   e: info@kellingheath.co.uk
alanrogers.com/UK3430   www.kellingheath.co.uk

Accommodation: ☑ Pitch ☑ Mobile home/chalet ○ Hotel/B&B ○ Apartment

Not many parks can boast their own railway station and Kelling Heath's own halt on the North Norfolk Steam Railway gives access to the beach at Sheringham. Set in 250 acres of woodland and heathland, this very spacious holiday park offers freedom and relaxation with 300 large, level, grass touring pitches, all with 16A electricity and six are fully serviced. Together with 384 caravan holiday homes (36 to let, the rest privately owned), they blend easily into the part-wooded, part-open heath. A wide range of facilities provides activities for all ages. 'The Forge' has an entertainment bar and a family room, with comprehensive entertainment all season. The leisure centre provides an indoor pool, spa pool, sauna, steam rooms and gym. An adventure playground with assault course is near. The central reception area is attractively paved to provide a village square with an open air bandstand where one can sit and enjoy the atmosphere.

You might like to know

Set amongst rare open heathland with backdrops of pine and native woodland. A magnificent range of facilities and environmental activities are offered for the whole family.

- ☑ Environmental accreditation
- ☑ Reduced energy/water consumption policy
- ☑ Recycling and reusing policy
- ☑ Information about walking and cycling
- ☑ Footpaths within 500 m. of the site
- ☑ Fishing within 1 km.
- ☑ Riding or pony trekking within 1 km.
- ○ Direct river or lake access
- ☑ Area of outstanding natural beauty or National Park within 10 km.
- ☑ Wildlife haven (on site or within 1 km)
- ☑ Public transport
- ☑ Dogs welcome

Rivendale Caravan & Leisure Park

Buxton Road, Alsop-en-le-Dale, Ashbourne DE6 1QU (Derbyshire)
t: 01335 310311   e: enquiries@rivendalecaravanpark.co.uk
alanrogers.com/UK3850   www.rivendalecaravanpark.co.uk

Accommodation: ☑ Pitch   ☑ Mobile home/chalet   ☑ Hotel/B&B   ○ Apartment

This unusual park has been developed in the bowl of a hill quarry which was last worked over 50 years ago. The steep quarry walls shelter three sides with marvellous views over the Peak District National Park countryside to the south. Near the entrance to the park is a renovated stone building which houses reception, shop, bar and a café/restaurant. Nearby are 102 level and landscaped pitches, mostly of a generous size with 16A electricity and a mix of hardstanding and grass. In two separate fields and a copse there is provision for 50 tents and that area includes a fishing lake. All the touring pitches are within easy reach of the central stone-built toilet block which is in keeping with the environment and provided with underfloor heating. A new lodge-style heated toilet block is at the entrance to the tent fields. For rent on the park are B&B rooms, camping pods, lodges and yurts.

You might like to know

Rivendale is an excellent location from which to view the night sky – the White Peak Astronomical Observing Group holds a Star Party at Rivendale twice a year.

- ☑ Environmental accreditation
- ☑ Reduced energy/water consumption policy
- ☑ Recycling and reusing policy
- ☑ Information about walking and cycling
- ☑ Footpaths within 500 m. of the site
- ☑ Fishing within 1 km.
- ○ Riding or pony trekking within 1 km.
- ☑ Direct river or lake access
- ☑ Area of outstanding natural beauty or National Park within 10 km.
- ○ Wildlife haven (on site or within 1 km)
- ○ Public transport
- ☑ Dogs welcome

Facilities: Good, heated toilet facilities include some washbasins in cubicles for ladies. Excellent en-suite room for disabled visitors. Laundry room. Motorcaravan services. Gas. Shop (all essentials). Bar (evenings) and café with homemade and local food (open mornings, lunch and evenings, w/ends only in low season). Special events monthly and games in main season. Hot tubs for hire, delivered to your pitch. Fly fishing lake. For rent are B&B rooms, camping pods, lodges and yurts. Two lodges adapted for wheelchair users. Torches useful. WiFi in some areas (charged). Off site: Riding and bicycle hire 5 miles. Sailing and boat launching 8 miles. Golf 10 miles. Alton Towers 35 minutes drive. Go Ape. National Tramway Museum. Chatsworth and Haddon Hall. Derwent Valley Mills.

Open: All year excl. 4-29 January.

Directions: Park is 7 miles north of Ashbourne on the A515 to Buxton, on the eastern side of the road. It is well signed between the turnings east to Alsop Moor and Matlock (A5012), but take care, this is a very fast section of the A515.
GPS: 53.106383, -1.760567

Charges guide

Per unit incl. 2 persons and electricity	£ 20.00 - £ 26.00
extra person	£ 2.50
child (4-15 yrs)	£ 2.00
dog	£ 2.00

Brynawelon Touring & Camping Park

Sarnau, Llandysul SA44 6RE (Ceredigion)
t: 01239 654584 e: info@brynaweloncp.co.uk
alanrogers.com/UK6005 www.brynaweloncp.co.uk

Accommodation: ☑ Pitch ☑ Mobile home/chalet ○ Hotel/B&B ○ Apartment

Paul and Liz Cowton have turned Brynawelon into a friendly, attractive and well appointed campsite. It is in a stunning rural location within two miles of the Ceredigion coast with its beaches, and close to the River Teifi with plenty of water based activities. All the 40 pitches have electricity hook-ups and of these, 25 are serviced hardstanding pitches (electricity, water and waste). A number of all-weather pitches for tents have been added recently. The remainder are on level grass. The park has ample room for children to play, an enclosed play area, an indoor games room with TV, and a sauna next to reception. Buzzards, red kites, owls and the occasional eagle can be seen from the park. There is also a wide variety of small birds. A wide choice of beaches can be found along the coast, there are dolphin trips from New Quay ten miles away and white water rafting on the Teifi at Llandysul. The Teifi is also a well known canoeing and fishing river.

You might like to know

Combining the delights of the countryside and the West Wales coast, this is a tranquil, unspoilt area. The local sandy beach and pretty village are ideal for a relaxing stroll.

○ Environmental accreditation
○ Reduced energy/water consumption policy
○ Recycling and reusing policy
☑ Information about walking and cycling
☑ Footpaths within 500 m. of the site
○ Fishing within 1 km.
○ Riding or pony trekking within 1 km.
○ Direct river or lake access
○ Area of outstanding natural beauty or National Park within 10 km.
☑ Wildlife haven (on site or within 1 km)
○ Public transport
☑ Dogs welcome

Facilities: Modern toilet block with toilets, showers, washbasins in cabins, two full suites in each side and a separate room for families and disabled visitors. Laundry/kitchen with washing machine, tumble dryer, ironing board and iron, fridge/freezer, microwave, kettle and toaster. Enclosed play area. Games room with table football, electronic games, TV and library. Sauna (charged). Dog walking area. WiFi (charged). Off site: Shops and pub 1 mile. Links with local farm shop (pre-order delivery, voucher scheme). Beach 1 mile. Fishing 2 miles. Golf and riding 3 miles. Dolphin trips at New Quay 10 miles. White-water rafting and canoeing at Llandysul 10 miles.

Open: March - 31 October.

Directions: Travelling north on the A487 from Cardigan turn right (southeast) at the crossroads in Sarnau village, signed Rhydlewis. Site is on the left after 650 yds. Note: the cross-country approach is not advised.
GPS: 52.13001, -4.45401

Charges guide

Per unit incl. 2 persons
and electricity £ 15.00

incl. 4 persons, hardstanding
and services £ 25.00

No credit cards.

Facilities: Toilet block (built in 2012) is spotlessly clean and has underfloor heating, family rooms, drying rooms, laundry, and spacious controllable showers. Reception stocks essentials. Campers' room with fridges and freezers, microwave, table and chairs. Fishing. Torches are useful. Free WiFi over site. Off site: Pub at Hundred House village 1 mile. Bicycle hire and golf 5 miles. Riding 7 miles.

Open: 1 March - 3 January.

Directions: Park is 4 miles east of Builth Wells near the village of Hundred House on A481. Follow brown signs. Do not use postcode on sat nav.

GPS: 52.17121, -3.31621

Charges guide

Per unit incl. 2 persons and electricity £ 20.00	
extra person (over 3 yrs) £ 3.00	
dog (max. 2) no charge	

No credit cards.

Fforest Fields Caravan & Camping Park

Hundred House, Builth Wells LD1 5RT (Powys)
t: 01982 570406   e: office@fforestfields.co.uk
alanrogers.com/UK6320   www.fforestfields.co.uk

Accommodation: ☑ Pitch ☑ Mobile home/chalet ○ Hotel/B&B ○ Apartment

This secluded park is set on a family hill farm within seven acres in the heart of Radnorshire. This is simple country camping and caravanning at its best, with no clubhouse, swimming pool or games room. The facilities include 80 large pitches on level grass on a spacious and peaceful, carefully landscaped field by a stream. Electrical connections (6-16A) are available and there are 17 hardstanding pitches, also with electricity. Several additional areas without electricity are provided for tents. There are two new lakes, one for boating and fly fishing, the other for coarse fishing. George and Katie, the enthusiastic owners, have opened up much of the farm for ample woodland and moorland trails which can be enjoyed with much wildlife to see. Indeed, wildlife is actively encouraged with nesting boxes for owls, songbirds and bats, by leaving field margins wild to encourage small mammals and by annual tree planting.

You might like to know

Why not try paragliding and experience the beauty of nature from the air!

○ Environmental accreditation
○ Reduced energy/water consumption policy
☑ Recycling and reusing policy
☑ Information about walking and cycling
☑ Footpaths within 500 m. of the site
○ Fishing within 1 km.
○ Riding or pony trekking within 1 km.
○ Direct river or lake access
○ Area of outstanding natural beauty or National Park within 10 km.
☑ Wildlife haven (on site or within 1 km)
○ Public transport
☑ Dogs welcome

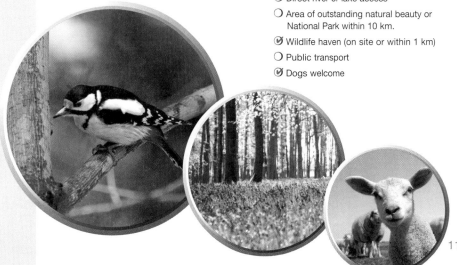

Facilities: The toilet block includes washbasins in cubicles and spacious hot showers. Two new cubicles with washbasin and WC. Separate laundry room and an en-suite unit for disabled visitors that doubles as a baby room, operated by key (£5 deposit). Outside covered area with fencing and concrete floor for dishwashing sinks and bins. Motorcaravan service point. Shop. Bicycle hire arranged. Caravan storage. WiFi (charged). 2 Romany-style caravans for rent. Off site: Fishing 200 yds. Boat launching, golf and riding 2 miles. Mon. market in Bala.

Open: 15 March - 27 October.

Directions: Park is 0.5 miles southeast of Bala village on the B4391. Bala is between Dolgellau and Corwen on the A494.

GPS: 52.901717, -3.590117

Charges guide

Per unit incl. 2 persons and electricity £ 19.00 - £ 23.00	
tent pitch incl. 2 persons £ 15.50 - £ 20.50	
extra person £ 7.50	
child (4-16 yrs) £ 4.00	
dog £ 1.00	

Pen-y-Bont Touring & Camping Park

Llangynog Road, Bala LL23 7PH (Gwynedd)
t: 01678 520549 e: penybont-bala@btconnect.co.uk
alanrogers.com/UK6340 www.penybont-bala.co.uk

Accommodation: ☑ Pitch ☑ Mobile home/chalet ○ Hotel/B&B ○ Apartment

This is a pretty little park with 59 touring pitches, 47 of which have hardstanding. Connected by circular gravel roads, they are intermingled with trees and tall trees edge the site. Electricity connections (16A) are available, including 11 for tents, and there are 28 serviced pitches with hardstanding, electricity, water and drainage. There are also pitches for 25 seasonal units. The park entrance and the stone building that houses reception and the well stocked shop provide quite a smart image. With views of the Berwyn mountains, Pen-y-bont has a peaceful, attractive and useful location being the closest park to Bala town. Bala Lake is 100 yards away and the park is three miles from the Welsh National White Water Centre, with Snowdonia on hand.

You might like to know

Bala Lake, close to the campsite, is the largest natural lake in Wales and offers all kinds of watersports and plenty of secluded spots to unwind.

- ○ Environmental accreditation
- ☑ Reduced energy/water consumption policy
- ☑ Recycling and reusing policy
- ☑ Information about walking and cycling
- ○ Footpaths within 500 m. of the site
- ☑ Fishing within 1 km.
- ○ Riding or pony trekking within 1 km.
- ○ Direct river or lake access
- ○ Area of outstanding natural beauty or National Park within 10 km.
- ☑ Wildlife haven (on site or within 1 km.)
- ○ Public transport
- ☑ Dogs welcome

Facilities: The four modern toilet blocks with showers (extra showers in two blocks) and units for visitors with disabilities. An excellent block in Nevis Park (one of the eight camping fields) has some washbasins in cubicles, showers, further facilities for disabled visitors, a second large laundry room and dishwashing sinks. Motorcaravan service point. Shop (Easter-mid Oct), barbecue area and snack bar (May-mid Sept). Play area on bark. Off site: Fishing 1 mile. Golf 4 miles. Riding 4.5 miles.

Open: 15 March - 31 October.

Directions: Turn off A82 to east at roundabout just north of Fort William following camp sign.

GPS: 56.804517, -5.073917

Charges guide

Per unit incl. 2 persons and electricity £ 16.50 - £ 22.50	
extra person £ 1.80 - £ 3.20	
child (5-15 yrs) £ 1.00 - £ 1.60	
dog no charge	

Glen Nevis Caravan & Camping Park

Glen Nevis, Fort William PH33 6SX (Highland)
t: 01397 702191 e: holidays@glen-nevis.co.uk
alanrogers.com/UK7830 www.glen-nevis.co.uk

Accommodation: ☑ Pitch ☑ Mobile home/chalet ○ Hotel/B&B ☑ Apartment

Just outside Fort William, in a most attractive and quiet situation with views of Ben Nevis, this spacious park is used by those on active pursuits as well as sightseeing tourists. It comprises eight quite spacious fields, divided between caravans, motorcaravans and tents (steel pegs required). It is licensed for 250 touring caravans but with no specific tent limits. The large touring pitches, many with hardstanding, are marked with wooden fence dividers, 174 with 13A electricity and 100 also have water and drainage. The park becomes full in the peak months but there are vacancies each day. If reception is closed (possible in low season) you site yourself. There are regular security patrols at night in busy periods. The park's own modern restaurant and bar with good value bar meals is a short stroll from the park, open to all. A well managed park with bustling, but pleasing ambiance, watched over by Ben Nevis.

You might like to know

The campsite is located at the foot of Ben Nevis, the highest mountain in the British Isles. There are numerous ways to discover this scenic area, including a gondola ride up Aonach Mor, a boat trip on Loch Linnhe or a day trip to Loch Ness.

○ Environmental accreditation
○ Reduced energy/water consumption policy
☑ Recycling and reusing policy
☑ Information about walking and cycling
☑ Footpaths within 500 m. of the site
☑ Fishing within 1 km.
☑ Riding or pony trekking within 1 km.
○ Direct river or lake access
○ Area of outstanding natural beauty or National Park within 10 km.
☑ Wildlife haven (on site or within 1 km)
○ Public transport
☑ Dogs welcome

Been to any good campsites lately?
We have

You'll find them here...

2015 · alan rogers · the best campsites **in Spain** & Portugal · over 300 independent reviews

2015 · alan rogers · the best campsites **in Netherlands** Belgium & Luxembourg · over 300 independent reviews

2015 · alan rogers · the best campsites **in Britain** & Ireland · over 800 independent reviews · FREE Travel Card

2015 · alan rogers · the best campsites **in Italy** Croatia & Slovenia · over 300 independent reviews

2015 · alan rogers · the best campsites **in France** · over 1000 independent reviews

the **BIG** selection **2015** · alan rogers · over 1000 independent reviews · the best campsites **in Europe** · FREE Travel Card

The UK's market leading independent
guides to the best campsites

... also here...

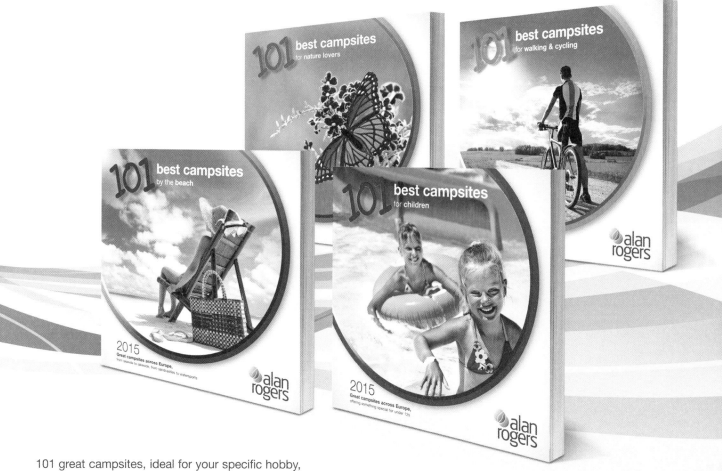

101 great campsites, ideal for your specific hobby,
pastime or passion

Want independent campsite reviews at your fingertips?

You'll find them here...

Over 3,000 in-depth campsite reviews at
www.alanrogers.com

...and even here...

Want to book your holiday on one of Europe's top campsites?

We can do it for you. No problem.

The best campsites in the most popular regions - we'll take care of everything

alan rogers travel

alan rogers

Discover the best campsites in Europe
with Alan Rogers

alanrogers.com
01580 214000

Index

Index

Index